Peter Ball is a freelance sports writer who
contributes to *The Times* and is the football
correspondent for Ireland's *Sunday Tribune*. He
started collecting sports quotes in the 1970s
when he was the sports editor of *Time Out* and in
1985 he began *The Times Sports Quotes of the
Year*. His books include *Only a Game?* with
Eamon Dunphy, *The Book of Cricket Quotations*
with David Hopps and *The Book of Football
Quotations* with co-author Phil Shaw. He is
married and has three sons.

Phil Shaw is a sports reporter for *The
Independent*. After working as a teacher,
librarian, market researcher and GLC clerk, he
entered journalism in the late 1970s with *Time
Out*, going on to work for *The Guardian* and *The
Observer*. As well as collaborating on *The Book of
Football Quotations*, now in its third edition, he
wrote *Whose Game Is It Anyway?*, a book about
football fanzines, which was published recently.
Phil is married and has two children.

Also by Peter Ball and Phil Shaw

The Book of Football Quotations

Peter Ball
Phil Shaw

SPORTS
QUOTES
OF THE
EIGHTIES

Mandarin

A Mandarin Paperback

SPORTS QUOTES OF THE EIGHTIES

First published 1990
by Mandarin Paperbacks
Michelin House, 81 Fulham Road, London SW3 6BR

Mandarin is an imprint of the Octopus Publishing Group

This collection copyright © Peter Ball and Phil Shaw 1990

A CIP catalogue record for this book
is available from the British Library
ISBN 0 7493 0366 2

Printed in Great Britain
by Cox & Wyman Ltd, Reading

Acknowledgements

Quotes don't just happen. Someone says them and, even more important, a journalist spots the jewel and records it. So our thanks are to the sportsmen and sportswomen who provided the material and, above all, to the journalists who waited in corridors and carparks for a 'quick word' with the heroes and villains of the hour.

More specific thanks are due to Frank Keating, who started the Cottage Industry, to Russell Thomas of *The Guardian* and Neil Morten of *The Independent* for their contributions, and to Keith Smith and Alison Rogers of *The Times* Picture Desk and Picture Library respectively, for their generous help.

All photographs are courtesy of Times Newspapers except the ones on pages 119 (Associated Press), 208 (Press Association) and 194 and 233 (*The Independent*).

Contents

1980

Evening lad, we can piss this y'know.
>**David Bairstow**, England wicketkeeper, to
>fellow-Yorkshireman Graham Stevenson on lat-
>ter's arrival at wicket at crucial stage in one-day
>international in Australia. England won.

●

It's part of the typical American prejudice that all
blacks love sports and all blacks can talk to each
other.
>**Tanzanian Government Official**, on Muhammad
>Ali's 'Boycott the Olympics' mission to Africa.

●

I'm the most recognised and loved man that ever lived.
There weren't no satellites when Jesus and Moses were
around, so people far away in the villages didn't know
about them.
>**Muhammad Ali.**

●

The only amateurs here are the organisers.
>**East German** official at the Winter Olympics
>in Lake Placid, USA.

●

Hell, we've been stockpiling our own snow since
November. That natural stuff'd just be a nuisance.
>**Robert F Flacke**, Parks Commissioner, at the
>Winter Games.

●

Perhaps I found our weakness at last.
>**Graham Turner**, Shrewsbury player-manager,
>after dropping himself from the team and seeing
>them win.

As the ball was fed out to Horton I went across to
try and charge down his kick. As I got close, Horton
turned his shoulder and I caught him in the face with
my right hand. I was really surprised when the referee
sent me off.

> **Paul Ringer**, Welsh forward, after the England-
> Wales rugby union match.

●

Paul is not a thug. He is kind, works hard and has
given his life to the game of rugby, which he loves.

> **Ringer's mother.**

●

It was like M*A*S*H in the medical room.

> **Leon Walkden**, Rugby Football Union doctor,
> after violent England v Wales international.

●

I thought we'd gone to Twickenham when the game
started. I thought the Welsh rugby team had taken
over.

> **Bob Paisley**, Liverpool manager, after bitter
> Merseyside derby.

●

People have been inventing things about me ever
since Twickenham. I was said to have shot a cow in
Brecon.

> **Paul Ringer.**

●

I'm not in, am I? Marvellous – bloody marvellous.

> **Paul Ringer** when recalled to the Wales XV.

●

I just want to get through this trip without being
quoted.

> **Brian Clough**, Nottingham Forest manager, on
> the European Cup trail in East Germany.

●

I might go to Alcoholics Anonymous, but I think
it'd be difficult for me to remain anonymous.

> **George Best**, admitting to booze problems after
> brief stay with Hibernian.

The crowd are literally electrified and glued to their seats.

Ted Lowe, TV snooker commentator.

●

When Peter scored the third goal I gave him a kiss and asked the umpire what he was going to do about it. He sent me off.

Nick Green, St Anne's hockey player sent off against Knutsford.

●

When St Anne's scored a very good second goal, the players over-reacted. I told them not to behave like footballers and got on with the game. But after the third goal Green defied what I had said.

John Machin, umpire.

●

I'm a light eater. As soon as it's light I start to eat.

Art Donovan, 310-lb former defensive lineman with Baltimore Colts American football team.

●

Of course I don't mind the fight being at three in the morning. Everyone in Glasgow fights at three in the morning.

Jim Watt, Scottish boxer.

●

I am frequently dismayed by the way golfers are turned out. Men dress badly, but women are worse. They turn up in old jeans or a crushed and tatty skirt they keep only for golf. It's not good enough and doesn't happen in other sports. It does not cost a lot to dress nicely, and if you are well turned out it can boost your ego and help you play better.

Joan Rothschild, organiser of the Avia Women's Tournament at Ascot, on why she was offering a prize for the best-dressed player.

●

You ought to get a bunch of clowns if you just want entertainment.

Alan Durban, Stoke City manager, replying to

3

critics of his side's negative display at Arsenal.

•

Eddie Waring has done for our game what Cyril
Smith has done for hang-gliding.

Reggie Bowden, Fulham rugby league player-
coach.

•

Football hooligans? Well there are the 92 club chairmen
for a start.

Brian Clough.

•

I have never been so insulted by anyone in football
as this little upstart.

Dennis Hill-Wood, Arsenal chairman, reacting
to Clough's remark.

•

The most violent offenders should be flogged in front
of the stand before home games. I feel so strongly on
this matter, I'd volunteer to do the whipping myself.

Allan Clarke, Leeds United manager, on hooliganism.

•

It sounds drastic, but the only way to stop the
hooligans is to shoot them.

Bobby Roberts, Colchester United manager.

•

There are more hooligans in the House of Commons
than at a football match.

Brian Clough warming to his theme.

•

My doctor told me jogging could add years to my
life. He was right – I feel 10 years older already.

Milton Berle, American comedian, on the jogging
craze.

•

Every time I get hit I want to quit the game. But
every time I hit it's a thousand dollars.

Sugar Ray Leonard, world welterweight boxing
champion.

I'm going down so often these days you'd think I was making a blue movie.

> **John Conteh**, British boxer, after defeat by Matthew Saad Muhammad.

●

I can close any cut in the world in 50 seconds, so long as it ain't a total beheading.

> **Adolph Ritacco**, Saad Muhammad's ex-corner man, after being banned for life for using illicit substances to repair injuries.

●

Trevor Brooking? He floats like a butterfly and stings like one too.

> **Brian Clough** before the FA Cup final, in which Brooking scored West Ham's winner against Arsenal.

●

I've watched thousands of fights but this one's beginning to turn my stomach. Antuofermo's face is just disintegrating.

> **Harry Carpenter**, BBC boxing commentator, on Minter v Antuofermo fight.

●

If you want Olympic Games, don't start Wars.

> **The Duke of Edinburgh.**

●

The Government is clutching at sport as a straw with which to beat the Russians.

> **Peter Lawson**, ITN.

●

I am not going to be used as a standard bearer by people on either side of the debate. In the end, this is a decision that must come from inside every individual, not from outside pressure.

> **Seb Coe**, British runner, on the Government call for the Moscow Games to be boycotted.

There are infinitely more important things in life than the Olympics, such as being loyal to one's country. I don't think the Russians should be allowed to get away with invading other people's countries. It's just not on, frankly.

Lucinda Prior-Palmer, British horse-woman, backing the British Equestrian Federation's decision to boycott the Olympic Games in Moscow.

If Seb doesn't win gold it will be defeat for him
but failure for me.
> **Peter Coe**, Seb's father, on coaching his son.
> •

Oh, do get some gold, it suits you so.
> **Emma Coe** in a letter to her brother in Moscow.
> •

We'll put that medal in a bottom drawer – if we
don't throw it away.
> **Peter Coe** after Seb's silver medal run in the 800m.
> •

One and three-quarter minutes of total disaster. That
was the one I came for.
> **Seb Coe** after the same race.
> •

I must go home and start my life all over again.
> **Tessa Sanderson**, British javelin-thrower, after
> failing to qualify for the final.
> •

We are the best middle-distance runners in the world
and I wish people would enjoy us as a team.
> **Steve Ovett** on his relations with British rival
> Seb Coe.
> •

I feel sorry for the Americans. They're supposed to be
the greatest democracy in the world yet nobody gets a
choice here.
> **Daley Thompson**, British decathlete, on the
> boycott.
> •

1980 will be the year when the world's politicians
will be able to sit down and say they successfully
dismantled sport.
> **Seb Coe**.
> •

Why stop something that's fun?
> **Daley Thompson** on whether he would retire
> after winning a decathlon gold medal.

The decathlon? Nine Mickey Mouse events and a 1,500 metres.

Steve Ovett.

●

Pity Ovett didn't show up. Then we could have had the good, the bald and the ugly.

Daley Thompson with Duncan Goodhew at a group-photo session of British gold winners in Moscow.

●

There is a Korean girl attempting double headsprings who I've never once seen land on her feet, always on her back. Imagine the effect on her spine later on in life. And all for an extra 0.5 marks. I don't think it's worth it any more.

Suzanne Dando, British gymnast, on why she was retiring.

●

I shouldn't be so upset at losing to Benfica. After all they have the best players, the best referees, and the best linesmen.

Jimmy Hagan, British manager of Portugal's Vitoria Setubal.

●

Three or four directors think I'm a good manager. It's not a question of whether they like me. I'm not a likeable person.

Bill McGarry before he was sacked as Newcastle manager.

●

He has the face of a choirboy, the demeanour of a Civil Servant and the ruthlessness of a rat-catcher.

Geoffrey Boycott on Kent and England bowler Derek Underwood.

●

What I'm now trying to get over to the public is that bobsleighing isn't solely populated by people from the gossip columns looking for a little exercise after another night in Annabel's.

Prince Michael of Kent.

●

Ten is a cruel age to lose your hair.

Duncan Goodhew, British swimmer.

●

There is no crisis at Crystal Palace.

Ray Bloye, the club chairman, as the 'Team of the Eighties' dropped to the bottom of the First Division.

●

Champions keep trying until they get it right.

Billie Jean King, American tennis player.

●

You're only here once, you know – it's not a rehearsal.

Malcolm Allison, football manager.

●

Our President tell army to play lugby. Is good training for soldiers.

Chong-Jen Chuang, secretary-general of the Republic of China RFU.

●

My gaad! I've got socks older than you.

Lee Trevino to a 27-year-old opponent, quoted by Peter Alliss in *Bedside Golf*.

●

The man in the street must wonder what's going on. He's queueing up for a cup of tea in the pouring rain at grounds where the amenities aren't good enough and all he reads about are £1 million transfers.

Gordon Taylor, Professional Footballers' Association secretary.

●

If I don't break my neck first, I'll get the hang of them.

Andrea Jaeger, American tennis player, after buying her first pair of high-heeled shoes.

I've had more comebacks than Frank Sinatra.
>   **Mike Hendrick**, England fast bowler, after taking
>   5 for 31 against Australia in a one-day match.

●

Sorry ref – I thought you were Garth Crooks.
>   **Vince Hilaire**, Crystal Palace footballer, to referee
>   Alf Grey after pushing him over during a match
>   against Spurs.

●

It would be a perfect way to go, except I don't
really plan to go just yet.
>   **Jack Nicklaus**, American golfer, after his surprise
>   win in the US Open.

●

I heard the news as I was driving to Queen's Club.
I nearly hit a car on my left and only just missed a
lamp-post on my right.
>   **John Feaver**, English tennis player, on hearing
>   he was drawn against Ilie Nastase at Wimbledon.

●

A lot of people were cheering me; it was probably
all the mothers I suppose.
>   **Evonne Cawley** of Australia after winning the
>   Wimbledon final.

●

They should send Bjorn Borg away to another planet.
We play tennis. He plays something else.
>   **Ilie Nastase**, Romanian tennis player.

●

Borg's won Wimbledon four straight times, and out
there he's just lost an 18–16 tie-breaker. You'd think
maybe just once he'd let up and just say 'forget it'. But
oh no, no way.
>   **John McEnroe**.

●

Tracy [Austin] just couldn't figure Evonne's game.
You see Tracy couldn't realise that Evonne flows; she
doesn't run like the rest of us, she just flows.
>   **Bob Landsdorp**, Miss Austin's coach.

I sigh with nostalgia for the days when at tournaments like Wimbledon the greatest danger to the chastity of young tennis stars came from randy males. Devastating, isn't it, to learn that nowadays their greatest peril would seem to come from other ladies in frilly panties.

> **John Junor** in his *Sunday Express* column.

●

This lesbian wedding gossip makes me mad. What bothers me is not so much what people say as the damage it could do to my endorsements [of products].

> **Martina Navratilova** on rumours that she had 'married' Rita Mae Brown.

●

You want I send my bodyguard to kill you?

> **Ilie Nastase** to reporters during Wimbledon.

●

If this is football, something's wrong.

> **John O'Hare**, Nottingham Forest substitute, during his team's 1–0 European Cup final victory over Hamburg when Forest played one up front.

●

The statistics suggest that he [Mike Brearley] is one of the great England captains. The luckiest would be nearer the truth.

> **Ray Illingworth**, former England cricket skipper.

●

My respect for Clough and [Peter] Taylor is genuine and I have too much regard for them to want to knife them in the back now I've left.

> **Garry Birtles** after his £1m transfer from Nottingham Forest to Manchester United.

●

We began thinking about replacing Birtles the moment we signed him. That's the way we always work.

> **Brian Clough**.

●

Press conferences are the curse of the modern game.

> **Bobby Robson**, Ipswich Town manager.

As far as cricket is concerned, Butcher is English now.
Alec Bedser, naming a West Indian, Roland Butcher, in the England cricket touring party.

●

A move like this only happens once in your life.
Clive Allen on joining Arsenal from QPR in June, two months before a second £1 million transfer, to Crystal Palace.

●

I believe that sport should exist and that because it exists the world is a bit better place.
Geoff Capes, British shot-putter.

●

At the end of the day, no matter who you are playing you get two points for a win, one for a draw and if you lose they laugh at you.
Ron Saunders, Aston Villa manager.

●

Tracy Austin was never the cute little kid that she looks.
Martina Navratilova.

●

Watching football on TV is like peeping through a keyhole.
Ron Greenwood, England manager.

●

I've always said there's a place for the Press but they haven't dug it yet.
Tommy Docherty, football manager.

●

Noah was an amateur; the Titanic was built by professionals.
Malcolm Allison on the right of Press 'amateurs' to criticise professional football people.

●

We've got a long-term plan at this club and except for the results it's going well.
Ernie Clay, Fulham FC chairman.

Conversation on a plane.
Stewardess: Mr Ali, please fasten your seat belt.
Muhammad Ali: Superman don't need no seat belt.
Stewardess: Superman don't need no plane, either.
  Quoted in *Sports Illustrated* magazine.

●

Any player who doesn't react must be a zombie or a
robot. If you can't laugh and you can't cry you might
as well die.
  Gordon Lee, Everton manager, on the FA's 'no
  kissing' request.

●

If we could get one against Forest I'd go out and
kiss and cuddle the scorer myself.
  Bob Paisley, Liverpool manager on the same
  subject.

●

Paolo Rossi disqualified for three years! I'd throw
myself out of the window if we were not on the
ground floor.
  Giussi Farina, President of Rossi's Italian football
  club, Vicenza.

●

Although we were beaten 24–9 I was not impressed
by the Springboks. They play a very negative game.
  Hugo Porta, Argentine rugby union fly-half.

●

I am petrified by snakes and all my life I have been
uneasy when walking alone in the dark. But fear in
a car? I never once felt it.
  Juan Manuel Fangio, racing driver.

●

In affectionate remembrance of English Cricket which
died at Lord's on September 2, 1980, aged one hundred.
The body will be re-cremated and sent to the home of
bureaucracy, officialdom, and the tactics of defensive
unadventurous cricket.
  Letter to *Wisden Cricket Monthly*.

Clive Lloyd's West Indians would have given
Bradman's 1948 'unbeatables' a real run for their
money. We'd have won, but only just.
> **Neil Harvey**, former Australian Test cricketer.

●

When I lost my world [decathlon] record I took it
like a man: I only cried for 10 hours.
> **Daley Thompson**.

●

If anyone wants my job they've got to take it away
from me over my dead body.
> **Ernie Walley**, Crystal Palace manager, Saturday
> November 29.

●

If I can work with anyone I can certainly work
with Malcolm.
> **Ernie Walley**, Sunday November 30, learning
> that he had been replaced by Malcolm Allison.

●

My strengths aren't half as good as her weaknesses.
> **Debbie Jeavons**, English tennis player, on losing
> 6–0, 6–0 to Chris Evert.

●

The ball game's over.
> **Angelo Dundee**, Muhammad Ali's trainer, after
> defeat by Larry Holmes.

●

Throughout the fight I was trying to pump him up.
But you can't pump up a torn tyre, just like you can't
get water out of a dry well.
> **Angelo Dundee**.

●

My sport is about 90 per cent strength and 40 per
cent technique.
> **Johnny Walker**, world middleweight wrist-
> wrestling champion.

My mind wasn't on the fight in the first round
and I didn't realise I'd been knocked down.
Charlie Magri, British boxer.

Now is the time for both players to relax, take their minds off the game, and just think about their tactics for the next set.

Anne Jones, BBC pundit, during Wimbledon.

●

The trouble with referees is that they just don't care which side wins.

Tom Canterbury, American basketball player.

●

Boxing has gone back a mile. There aren't enough tradesmen because there isn't enough competition and if it wasn't for the coloured fellows there wouldn't be any boxing in this country.

Eddie Thomas, Welsh promoter.

●

I told him I thought he had more sense than to take on that job at his age.

Brian Clough on his conversation with new Labour Party leader Michael Foot.

●

When do you ever see a player smile these days? I don't go to a football ground to experience misery. I go along to forget the rest of the week and enjoy myself.

Jimmy Hill, TV football presenter.

●

Don't forget that nobody forces people to box. They do it because they want to, because they are dedicated to the sport.

Adrian Whiteson, Board of Control doctor.

●

They could put ten dustbins out there and do the job they do.

Terry McDermott of Liverpool on Nottingham Forest's tactics.

●

I don't understand money, it baffles me. I don't know the value of paper things in a wallet. My accountant

doesn't trust me with a cheque book or credit card.
   Malcolm Allison.

   ●

If it wasn't for golf, I'd be a caddie today.
   George Archer, pro golfer.

   ●

The French cannot produce great track and field
teams like they can produce great wines for probably
that very reason; the winemakers got in first.
   Michael Lourie, French national coach.

   ●

I'm on a seafood diet. It means I eat everything
I can see.
   Competitor in New York Marathon.

   ●

Whenever I'm away from Derry for more than two or
three days I am desperate to get back. And I've never
got home and it hasn't been raining.
   Charlie Nash, Irish boxer.

   ●

There are two things not long for this world – dogs
that chase cars and pro golfers who chip for pars.
   Lee Trevino, American golfer.

   ●

Bowles has burned his bridges, his boats and anything
else that floats.
   Brian Clough on the errant Stanley.

   ●

He's about a stone and a half overweight and has
been told to get it off.
   Alec Bedser on England cricket captain Ian
Botham.

   ●

It's not the fault of my cooking. He gets no potatoes,
stodgy pudding or anything that's fattening. He simply
hasn't played enough cricket. It's the weather.
   Kathryn, Botham's wife.

   ●

If all English cricket's got to worry about is my

weight then it must be in a strange way.
Ian Botham
●

Deryck Murray has batted well: he is the nigger
in the woodpile as far as the English are concerned.
Brian Johnston, BBC cricket commentator.
●

The Coloured kids are sad and aware that the Lions
being here means Britain has forsaken them. When I
watch the Lions on television my two teenage sons, who
love sport, get up and go quietly to their room and play
sad music.
Hassan Howa, president of non-white South
African Cricket Board.
●

I will not allow my son to play [with blacks]. Besides,
he has told me himself that he would rather give up
rugby than scrum down with them.
F J Meintjies, leading South African National
Party member, on the 'relaxation' of Apartheid
laws.
●

West Wales breed the fly-halves, the Gwent valleys
produce the mighty forwards.
Carwyn James, journalist and former Welsh
rugby union player.
●

In this game all you need is speed, strength and
an ability to recognise pain immediately.
Reggie Williams, Cincinnati Bengals linebacker.
●

In my first marathon I got excited, even euphoric. It
was a feeling I never had on the track. On the road
competitors hand around sponges. In a 5,000 all they
give you are elbows.
Dick Quax, New Zealand distance runner.
●

Sir, – An electrician recently came into my office to
mend the fire alarm. Finding a broken wire he said

'Look at this, it's kerried'. I asked what he meant and he replied 'It's Kerry Packered – knackered!'
> Letter in *Wisden Cricket Monthly*.

●

One reason that Finland produces such great runners is that back home it costs $2.40 a gallon for gas.
> **Esa Tikkanen**, Finnish marathon runner.

●

When I go along for a quiet evening's entertainment throwing beer cans I do not expect my enjoyment to be ruined by the sight of two grown men beating the living daylights out of each other.
> Letter to *The Guardian*.

●

All the team are 100 per cent behind the manager, but I can't speak for the rest of the squad.
> **Brian Greenhoff**, Leeds United player, on BBC Radio Leeds.

●

When I'm thwarted in show business I say to myself it's no worse than a crosscourt drive in squash – and I know how to deal with them.
> **Tommy Steele**.

●

On Saturday May 27 at Headingly, Yorkshire dismissed Lancashire at 12.47 p.m. for 123, the innings having lasted for 27.1 overs. Is this the highest score any side has been dismissed for before lunch on the first day of a county match. Yours, etc., Malcolm Thomas, Leeds.
> Letter to *Wisden Cricket Monthly*.

●

I prefer golf to tennis; all tennis courts look alike.
> **Brad Dillman**.

●

We talked long and hard about this possible problem but we decided there wasn't one.
> **Alec Bedser**, chairman of Test selectors.

1981

Athletes in Action [evangelical basketball team] beat you up in the first half, pray for you at half-time, then beat you up in the second half.

Jerry Tarkanian, University of Nevada-Las Vegas coach, after a heavy defeat.

•

I've just one ambition left, I reckon. To have one innings early on in the Tests and see the buggers take the new ball. That's what I want, and I'll bore them to death if needs be.

Geoffrey Boycott before England's cricket tour to the West Indies.

•

My problems are all behind me.

Ken Brett, Kansas City basketball player, on suffering from piles.

•

My word, you need to be fit to play this game!

Tony Green commentating on the British Open Darts Championship at Stoke-on-Trent.

•

We're halfway round the Grand National course with many hurdles to clear. So let's make sure we keep our feet firmly on the ground.

Mike Bailey, Charlton football manager, on his team's promotion prospects.

•

Cox are cox no matter what sex they are.

Oxford Union president on the University's woman cox in the Boat Race.

•

Why not? Wouldn't you go to China or Russia if

it was a free tip with all expenses paid?

Geoffrey Boycott on why he would still go to South Africa.

●

Forgetting politics, South Africa is the best country in the world in which to play rugby, and the hospitality is second to none.

Graham Price, Welsh rugby union international.

●

They offered me a handshake of £10,000 to settle amicably. I told them they would have to be a lot more amicable than that.

Tommy Docherty on being sacked as manager of Preston North End.

●

Born in Italy, most of his fights have been in his native New York.

Desmond Lynam, BBC boxing commentator.

●

There's only one thing I can say after that over, and that's to clap my hands.

Trevor Bailey, BBC Radio Three cricket summariser.

●

When I said: 'You're a disgrace to mankind,' I was talking to myself, not you.

John McEnroe to umpire Wing Commander George Grime at Wimbledon.

●

Vultures.

John McEnroe to the crowd on the Centre Court.

●

Shush.

John McEnroe to the committee tea-room at Queen's Club.

●

Mr McEnroe called me a four-letter word. It was not a very serious one.

Fred Hoyles, Wimbledon referee.

Shut up.
   John McEnroe to the crowd at the French Open.
   ●
Fame has not gone to his head. If there is anyone
with a great deal of humility it is John McEnroe.
   John McEnroe Snr.
   ●
I get screwed up by the umpires in this place.
   John McEnroe at Wimbledon.
   ●
Mr McEnroe, I must warn you that you are abusing
your racket. Please behave.
   Edward James, Wimbledon umpire.
   ●
I am not having points taken off me by an incompetent
old fool. You are the pits of the world.
   John McEnroe to Wimbledon umpire Edward
   James.
   ●
I am so disgusting you shouldn't watch. Everybody
leave.
   John McEnroe after missing a shot.
   ●
You must arrest him, he's the worst umpire I've
ever seen.
   John McEnroe to a policeman at Wimbledon.
   ●
Nothing any member of my family does surprises
me any more.
   Mrs Hunt, mother of James, on hearing her
   son David also wanted to be a race driver.
   ●
The sun always seemed to burn from a cloudless sky
at The Oval, dark blue except where it was streaked
by the white trail of a passing jet.
   Christopher Martin-Jenkins in his introduction
   to the *Wisden Book of County Cricket*.

I don't think I've done any permanent damage.
   Graham Marsh, Australian golfer, after playing
   a shot while sitting on a barbed wire fence.
        ●
If I was starting today, I think I'd take up snooker
and darts professionally. That's where the money is.
   Joe Hulme, former Arsenal footballer, at 76.
        ●
Just because the weather is cold there is no need to
appear in public like a sack of potatoes. All it needs is
some thermal underwear.
   Sponsor's letter to competitors in women's golf
   tournament.
        ●
I don't think I deserved to be dropped. I think a lot
of people in Wales and further afield will be surprised
and perhaps upset when they hear the news.
   J.P.R. Williams on being left out of the Wales
   rugby union team.
        ●
Even the Yorkshire Ripper got a fair trial but I've
never been given a single chance.
   Geoffrey Boycott on being overlooked as England
   cricket captain.
        ●
We should give the game back to the players; they've
had everything else.
   Ron Atkinson, Manchester United manager.
        ●
I told the selectors that if they were not prepared to
give me the job for the rest of the series I would not
wish to carry on.
   Ian Botham on giving up the England captaincy.
        ●
First thing I'm going to do is get these teeth
straightened.
   Jimmy White, 19 years old, after signing a
   lucrative snooker contract.

Athletics should not be about times but about finishing first.

Seb Coe.

●

We will have to play very badly and England very well to mess it up now.

Kim Hughes, Australian cricket captain, halfway through the third Test.

●

We did nothing wrong in the match except lose it.

Kim Hughes after England had won the third Test.

●

Everybody likes to be liked.

Kerry Packer, quoting his father.

●

In Czechoslovakia there is no freedom of the Press and in England there is no freedom from the Press.

Martina Navratilova, US-based Czech tennis player.

●

Can't you speak English?

John McEnroe to an umpire in the French Open.

●

When I think of Torquay it saddens me. There is no culture there at all. It's a musical desert.

Charles Ernesco, 76-year-old one-time classical violinist, after trying to win the seniors' golf championship.

●

I quite enjoyed it until I found out the author commmitted suicide.

Nick Job, golfer, after reading a book on the power of positive thinking.

●

I have a cheque for $16,000 but I feel I should give half of it back.

Martina Navratilova after Chris Evert beat her 6–0, 6–0 in a US tournament.

It is not helping our game when players go on the pitch thinking about how much they can earn instead of how to win matches.

Bert Millichip, FA chairman, after England's World Cup defeat by Norway.

●

Footballers tend to stay in the game because they can't do anything else. Some never learn that society doesn't owe them a living.

Ray Wilson, 1966 World Cup-winner, now an undertaker in Huddersfield.

●

Despite his problems he is still the world's most exciting player.

Chris Evert, American tennis player, on her husband John Lloyd.

●

The tackling in international soccer is frightening. Even a nation like the Swiss, not noted for ruthlessness, have joined in.

Geoff Hurst, assistant to England manager Ron Greenwood.

●

Hopefully the combination of relaxed thinking and just taking things as they come will help me relax so I can become consistently better.

Ed Plucknett, US discus thrower and world-record holder, a week before he was banned for life for taking steroids.

●

To be fair, they were on strange ponies. It's like going out with a new woman – you always take it easy first time.

Robert Graham, England's polo captain, excusing Spain's 10–5 defeat on borrowed ponies.

●

Not everyone should be like Connors, Nastase and McEnroe, but not everybody should be like Borg either. All McEnroe does is complain. Does he kill anybody?

What does he do that is so horrible? I tell you, they
were out to get him this year.

> **Ilie Nastase** after more trouble involving McEnroe
> in the US Open.

●

I'm this side of the line, you're that side and never
the twain shall meet. If they do I'll break your teeth.

> **Rodney Marsh**, Australian wicketkeeper, to a
> spectator who fielded a ball inside the boundary
> rope.

●

He wouldn't have said that to me later in the day
after I'd had a drink or two.

> The spectator.

●

I knew he would never play for Wales; he's tone deaf.

> **Vernon Davies** on hearing that his son Huw
> had been chosen for the England rugby union
> squad.

●

Playing with wingers is more effective against European sides like Brazil than English sides like Wales.

> **Ron Greenwood**, England football manager.

●

I learned a long time ago that minor surgery is
when they do the operation on someone else, not you.

> **Bill Walton**, American basketball player.

●

Any other sport would give its right arm to be as
unhealthy as people tell us football is.

> **Brendan Foster**, English long-distance runner.

●

Now it is going to be a Charles-and-Diana situation.

> **Bert Patrick**, head of England football kit-makers,
> Admiral, after the team scraped into the World Cup
> finals.

●

Some of the people who have been picked for England

Don't try to change him or the way he plays.
Do that and you've lost your chance of winning
Test matches.
   Kim Hughes on Ian Botham.

recently should have written back to the FA saying 'There must be some mistake; I can't play'.

Raich Carter, former England footballer.

•

Last winter I broke my back, which kept me out for a bit, but I've had nothing serious.

Michael Lee, 1980 speedway champion.

•

I don't know what they've got against my wife. She never played rugby league.

David Watkins, former rugby union international, on hearing he was not welcome at Cardiff's annual dinner.

•

A manager must buy cheap and sell dear. Another manager rings me to ask about a player. 'He's great' I say, 'super lad, goes to church twice a day, good in the air, two lovely feet, make a great son-in-law'. You never tell them he couldn't trap a bag of cement.

Tommy Docherty.

•

People from Los Angeles have come here asking for advice now that they've gotten the Games for 1984. I've told them my first piece of advice is 'Give 'em back'.

Rev Bernard Fell, Lake Placid Olympic Organising Committee.

•

I got my title crack all right – on the chin.

Charlie Magri after being knocked out by Juan Diaz.

•

You always get problems in a football club.

Terry Neill, Arsenal manager.

•

I was joyous and I did cry and laugh at the same time and I thanked the kind Lord of being so good to an old lady.

Mrs Marie Stuart, grandmother of Barbados-born cricketer Roland Butcher, on hearing he was chosen to play for England.

●

A short speech should be like a mini-skirt – short
enough to attract attention but long enough to cover
the bare essentials.

> **The Duke of Edinburgh** on being told he
> could address the Olympic Congress for only
> three minutes.

●

Tennis players are a load of wankers. I'd love to
put McEnroe in the centre for Fulham and let some
of those big rugby players sort him out.

> **Colin Welland**, playwright/writer and Fulham
> rugby league director.

●

Given a choice between Raquel Welch and a hundred
at Lord's I'd take the hundred every time.

> **Geoffrey Boycott**.

●

All through that last fight I kept saying to myself 'What
am I doing here? I should be in Tramps enjoying myself
not getting knocked about by this madman [Matthew
Saad Muhammad]'.

> **John Conteh** announcing his (first) retirement
> from the ring.

●

I have not read the Gleneagles Agreement. The only
thing I know about Gleneagles is that it has a good
golf course.

> **Alec Bedser**, chairman of England's cricket
> selectors, on the controversy over Robin Jackman,
> who had played in South Africa, being called up to
> play in the West Indies.

●

My line isn't on the job.

> **Ron Greenwood** after England's defeat by Spain.

●

Sometimes I wish his dad had taken him [Eric

Bristow] to Sunday school instead of down the pub.
Tony Brown, darts player.

●

Wimbledon is fantastic – different to any other
tournament in the world. The spectators are very
reserved and everyone wants the underdog to win.
Buster Mottram, British tennis player, according
to the *Sunday Times*, 21 June.

●

Wimbledon is a national disgrace, a farce. While kids
struggle to beat the odds, learning to play on poor
park courts with make-do facilities, the All-England
members enjoy cheap whisky, subsidised meals and
almost-free tennis balls.
Buster Mottram, according to the *Sunday Mirror*,
21 June.

●

And there's the unmistakable figure of Joe Mercer
. . . or is it Lester Piggott?
Brough Scott, TV racing commentator.

●

We had cricket for breakfast, dinner and tea. It
was like an obsession bordering on madness. He could
tell you who scored what years ago – and even what
the weather was like. But he could not remember my
birthday unless I reminded him.
Mildred Rowley, on her divorce from her husband
Mike, the Stourbridge CC scorer.

●

Cricket always came first for me. I wouldn't go to
my daughter's confirmation or my grand-daughter's
christening. They clashed with cricket. I did go to my
mother-in-law's funeral though. I'd sooner spend my
time scoring cricket than with my wife.
Mike Rowley.

●

[Manchester] United have begun to think that 'class'

is something which comes with big office suites and flash cars.

Harry Gregg, former United goalkeeper, after his sacking from a coaching job at the club.

●

That great club is slowly being destroyed, and I blame one family for the ruin. The Edwards family. The master butchers of Manchester.

Harry Gregg.

●

I'd rather face Dennis Lillee with a stick of rhubarb than go through all that again.

Ian Botham after being cleared of a night-club assault at Grimsby Crown Court.

●

Geoffrey Boycott is a giant playing among pygmies.

Peter Briggs, leader of Yorkshire cricket members' Reform Group.

●

The sort of tackle that got him [Paul Ringer] sent off at Twickenham happens in every rugby league match. He's a big, tough lad but no more vicious than a lot of players in our game.

Jim Mills, sent off 21 times in his rugby league career, on Ringer's arrival in the professional ranks.

●

All my life I wanted to play like Jack Nicklaus and now I do.

Paul Harvey, ABC-TV commentator, on Nicklaus's round of 83 at The Open.

●

The amateur system is an insult to my ego and intelligence. It's insulting to me to have to exist like this. People in the sport feel like they're doing something illegal just trying to survive.

Ed Moses, American 400m hurdles world-record holder.

Experienced professionals don't have to start buggering about with this gamesmanship lark. That's for amateurs.

Brian Barnes, British golfer.

•

When I look at someone like Henry Cooper, who is a very nice fellow but doesn't have a particularly interesting or colourful personality, I think 'if he can get on, why can't I?'

Brian Jacks, British judo international.

•

It's like having a jug full of wine with a tiny spout. It's there but we're not getting it.

San Francisco soccer promoter on the failure of the US to produce world-class talent.

•

My dad came to the United States two years ago but after three days he said 'My God, what is this place?' and went home.

Hana Mandlikova, Czech tennis player.

•

It's a funny thing about athletics that you put so much into every day that you find out a lot about yourself. I always wanted to be a star. Now I find it's not for me. I just want to be an athlete again.

Daley Thompson.

•

One of the best day's Test cricket we have had for a long while – a magic day.

Kim Hughes, Australian captain, during the fourth Test.

•

I just can't put my finger on the reason why we lost it.

Kim Hughes at the end of the fourth Test.

•

I have consistently interpreted Law 26 on 'misconduct' by awarding a scrum for obscenity and a penalty for blasphemy.

Alec C. Charters, chaplain and deputy head-

master of a Leatherhead school in a letter to
The Times.

●

It was an 'aw' game. We were awful and they were
awesome.
American basketball coach after 51–74 defeat.

●

Let's be honest, we're all out to cut each other's throats.
John Bond, Manchester City manager.

●

I owe everything to golf. Where else could a guy
with an IQ like mine make this much money?
Hubie Green, American golfer.

●

Some managers are difficult to deal with these days.
Everyone is money-mad.
Terry Neill, Arsenal manager.

●

I don't know if I've been patient or just stubborn.
Peter Oosterhuis, British golfer, after winning
the Canadian Open, his first win in seven years
on the US circuit.

●

If Sibson hits Alan on the chin with a left, Alan
will hit him back harder with a right.
Doug Bidwell, Alan Minter's manager, before
Minter v Sibson fight.

●

I felt great but he just hit me one on the whiskers.
Alan Minter after being knocked out in the
third round.

●

In the Bob Hope Golf Classic the participation of
President Gerald Ford was more than enough to
remind you that the nuclear button was at one stage
at the disposal of a man who might have either pressed
it by mistake or else pressed it deliberately in order to
obtain room service.
Clive James.

No I never broke my nose playing ice hockey; but eleven other guys did.

Gordie Howe, American player.

●

It was Jung, I think, who said we learned from our failures, success merely confirming us in our mistakes. What can I learn from my batting failures at Test level?

Mike Brearley, former England cricket captain.

●

McEnroe was especially irascible, and shouted assorted unprintables thirteen different times before earning another on-court audience with the referee. Lady Diana Spencer left the Royal Box during the match. 'The wedding's off,' someone said. 'Her ears are no longer virgin.'

Sports Illustrated.

●

Grand Double Horror Bill Tonight: *Jaws 2* and England v Switzerland soccer.

Notice outside Glasgow video theatre.

●

Rally points scoring is 20 points for the fastest, 18 for the second fastest, right down to six points for the slowest fastest.

Murray Walker, BBC motor-sport commentator.

●

In a pub, worse than the 'buttonholer' is the 'expert'. There's a terribly self-satisfied little jerk in the Coach and Horses – he calls himself an advertising executive, whatever that means – who was telling us the other day that Botham doesn't hold his bat correctly. He then addressed Mr Botham himself on the television screen and told him to adjust his left hand. He has even given Mr Piggott riding instructions.

Jeffrey Bernard, journalist and punter.

●

Judgments by commentators should be made on probability, not outcome. So when Jim Laker writes

If you want to interest Frenchmen in a
sport, you tell them it's war. And if you want
to interest the British in a war, you tell them
it's a game.

Jean-Pierre Rives, French rugby union
captain.

in the *Express* on Friday that it was a mistake to put
Australia in to bat at The Oval, one should know that
his opinion (given to Paul Parker's father) an hour
before the start on Thursday was that we should field.
And it is facile to refer to playing only four specialist
bowlers as 'folly' only after three of them have broken
down.

Mike Brearley.

●

She's dragged the javelin back into the twentieth
century.

Ron Pickering, BBC athletics commentator.

●

To me, life in big-time tennis means carrying large
amounts of small change in different currencies to
work laundromats wherever I happen to be. I spend
more time at nights watching my smalls go round than
I do watching television.

Sue Barker, English tennis player.

●

And that's the third time this session he's missed
his waistcoat pocket with the chalk.

Ted Lowe, BBC snooker commentator.

●

Yurgggh! Der stod Ingelland. Lord Nelson! Lord
Beaverbrook! Winston Churchill! Henry Cooper! Clem-
ent Attlee! Anthony Eden! Lady Diana! Der stod dem
all! Der stod dem all! Maggie Thatcher, can you hear
me? Can you hear me Maggie? Your boys take one hell
of a beating tonight.

Borg Lillelien, Norwegian World Cup commentator.

●

The BBC did not apologise to viewers who were
deprived of seeing half of Botham's century on
Saturday at Old Trafford because somebody in his
wisdom decided precedence should be taken by a

horserace from Newbury and the Midland Bank Horse Trials.

Richard Ingrams, editor of *Private Eye*.

●

It is all just physically and mentally soul-destroying.

Geoffrey Boycott.

1982

Some of our players can hardly write their names
– but you should see them add up.
Karl-Heinz Thielan, former general manager of
FC Cologne.

●

Half a million for Remi Moses? You could get the
original Moses and the tablets for that price.
Tommy Docherty, ex-Manchester United manager, on his old club's signing from West Bromwich.

●

I owe a lot to my parents, especially my mum and dad.
Greg Norman, Australian golfer.

●

You're the best supporters in the country and we're
the most attack-minded team.
Allan Clarke to the Leeds United crowd – four
days before they were relegated.

●

He floats like an anchor, stings like a moth.
Ray Gandolf, US TV commentator, on
Muhammad Ali at 39.

●

Leaving out Dennis Lillee against England would
be as unthinkable as the Huns dropping Attilla.
Australian cricket commentator.

●

Can you verbalise your emotions?
US reporter's request to Martina Navratilova
after she had won Wimbledon.

●

I don't know which language to protest in.
Navratilova in Montreal when all the announce-
ments were in French and English.

Dying is no big deal, the least of us will manage
that. Living is the trick.
> **Red Smith**, American sports writer's philosophy
> recalled in his own obituary.

●

The pitch is a great leveller.
> **Mike Bailey**, Brighton manager, after a 0–0
> draw on Barnet's sloping pitch in the FA Cup.

●

Unfortunately we have tended to take rugby too
seriously and perhaps too negatively. If you have
to lose, lose gracefully without recriminations and
inquests. The game is there to be enjoyed.
> **Hermas Evans**, Wales RU president.

●

He wants Texas back.
> **Tommy Lasorda**, Los Angeles Dodgers' baseball
> manager, on contractual demands of his Mexican-
> born star Fernando Valenzuela.

●

Television is a confounded nuisance, with gangs of
scruffy men wandering about ruining the occasion.
> **Peter Coni QC**, chairman of the Henley Rowing
> Regatta.

●

Colin may not have looked too good, but I'm told
he smelled lovely.
> **Steve Smith**, England rugby union captain,
> on prop Colin Smart's collapse after drinking
> aftershave at post-match banquet in Paris.

●

It was about par for a rugby dinner . . . from what
I remember.
> **Colin Smart**.

●

The aftershave will flow tonight.
> **Steve Smith** after victory over Wales a month
> later.

And Wilkins sends an inch-perfect pass to no one
in particular.
>   **Bryon Butler**, BBC Radio Two football commen-
>   tator.

●

Watford are setting English football back 10 years.
>   **Terry Venables**, Queen's Park Rangers manager,
>   on Watford's success with the long-ball game.

●

If Watford could put the game back 10 years it
would be in a better state than it is now.
>   **Danny Blanchflower**, former Spurs and Northern
>   Ireland captain.

●

It's obvious these Soviet swimmers are determined
to do well on American soil.
>   **Anita Lonsborough**, BBC-TV swimming com-
>   mentator.

●

The time-outs smell better.
>   **Butch van Breda Kolff**, basketball coach, on
>   why he left a men's team in the US to coach
>   a women's one.

●

That's the last thing I want, to finish the season with
a defeat. And I have every confidence we will achieve
it.
>   **Terry Russell**, Crayford speedway promoter,
>   before the match against Milton Keynes. Crayford
>   won by a League record 76–20.

●

I used to live opposite the Aintree course and the main
interest the local people had in the Grand National was
in hiring out their driveways as parking space for the
Range Rovers of the rich people who came up for the
race.
>   **Barry Woodward**, Merseyside County Council
>   public relations officer.

It was a lovely picture. She had her arms
out – like the Pope.
   Erika Roe's father after her 'streak' during rugby international at Twickenham.

I would have given my right arm to have been a pianist.
Bobby Robson on what he would like to have achieved had he not been a success in football.
•

If we had given them everything they asked for, England would have been out for single figures in each innings and Pakistan would have scored 500 runs in one. They obviously expected a favourable decision on all their appeals, but when 99 per cent are ridiculous and are turned down, the atmosphere becomes edgy and life becomes difficult, if not impossible, for umpires.
Ken Palmer after umpiring the first Test at Edgbaston.
•

Of course I'm gonna bloody ride again. It wasn't my fault I fell off.
Barry Sheene, motor-cycle ace.
•

We are capable of beating anybody, but equally we are never certain of avoiding defeat.
Miljan Miljanic, Yugoslavia football manager.
•

Let's be honest. A proper definition of an amateur today is one who accepts cash not cheques.
Jack Kelly Jnr, US Olympic Committee vice-president.
•

We play a man-to-man defense. Person-to-person sounds like a telephone call.
Basketball coach at Belmar, New Jersey Girls' High School.
•

It's all right for the British Medical Association to talk about banning boxing. They have a qualified living. I've no qualifications. No job. Boxing is the best thing I do. It's really all I know.
Erroll Christie, British middleweight.

The whole situation stinks. That could easily be me next time.

> **Ray Mancini**, world lightweight champion, after the death of opponent Duk Koo Kim.

●

There is about as much chance of this Super League idea getting through as there is of Arthur Scargill admitting he needs a wig.

> **Ernie Clay**, chairman of Fulham FC.

●

We are pulling out because we are a clean and upright company – something that can no longer be said of football. It is a sick sport. We would rather sponsor netball.

> **Malcolm Stanley**, managing director of FADS, D-I-Y retailers, on their withdrawal from a deal with Charlton.

●

[Norman] Cowans should remember what happened to [Graham] Dilley, who started out as a genuinely quick bowler. Then they started stuffing 'line' and 'length' into his ear, and now he has Dennis Lillee's action with Denis Thatcher's pace.

> **Geoffrey Boycott**.

●

Anyone who can organise something as magnificent as this [the All England Championship] is just the sort of person Sandy Woodward would have liked to have with him in the South Atlantic.

> **Max Robertson** striking a Falklands note at Wimbledon.

●

When I said even my Missus could save Derby County from relegation, I was exaggerating.

> **Peter Taylor**, no longer Brian Clough's partner, tasting failure.

[Brian] Clough talks in riddles. He says things like
'If you were half as flamboyant on the pitch as you
are off it, you'd be a world-beater.'

Justin Fashanu, Nottingham Forest's £1m striker
from Norwich, out of favour with his new manager.

●

I understand Fashanu took his own masseur to the
ground, and that is something I cannot condone.

Gordon Taylor, secretary of the footballers'
union, on Fashanu's ban from Forest's training
HQ.

●

I hit him. What more could I do?

Frank Bruno after one of his characteristically
quick wins, a 40-second KO of Gilbert Acuna.

●

Manchester United offered me a really excellent
contract. But what City offered was far in excess.
I couldn't believe it . . . it was much too high.

Trevor Francis, England footballer, on his move
from Nottingham Forest.

●

It remains to be seen whether blacks have what it
takes to adapt to the rigours of tennis. We are always
hearing how good they are at sprinting and jumping,
but apart from [Arthur] Ashe and Althea Gibson, there
hasn't been one who has risen to the top. Maybe it has
something to do with nature.

Phillippe Chatrier, president of the International
Tennis Federation.

●

It is an assumption he made. He made a mis-statement.

Paulo Angelli, Chatrier's special assistant.

●

As long as Oleg Blokhin plays, we will need him
here. When we don't need him any more I don't think
anyone else will be interested.

Vyacheslav Koloskov, Soviet football president,

denying reports that Blokhin would be transferred
to a Western club.

●

It is a case of the movable object against the resistible
force.

John Newman, manager, as his Derby side who
had lost their last 11 away games prepared to visit
Grimsby, who then had the worst home record in
the league. Grimsby won 1–0.

●

I'm not just involved in tennis, I am committed to it.
Do you know the difference? Think of ham and eggs
. . . the chicken is involved, the pig is committed.

Martina Navratilova.

●

He's not only a good player, but he's spiteful in
the nicest sense of the word.

Ron Atkinson, manager, on Manchester United's
teenage striker Norman Whiteside.

●

He's had a three-week holiday in Florida since the
World Cup. How does he think a miner feels in January
having to get up for the early shift at 6am?

Terry Neill, Arsenal manager, unimpressed when
his full-back Kenny Sansom said he might be tired
by January after playing for England in the World
Cup.

●

If we are here, we are here to compete against
all teams. Football is not a neutron bomb.

Konstantin Beskov, Soviet Union manager, at
the World Cup group draw in Madrid.

●

The referee was shameless but I'd better be quiet.
My country hasn't any money and can't pay fines.

Daniel Matamoros after Honduras had lost 1–0
to Yugoslavia through a late penalty in the World
Cup finals in Spain.

It's all clean dancing, we just wiggle and things.
> Topless disco dancer introduced to the England
> football team as a member of a ballet troupe.

●

Don't worry lads, Ally McLeod's in Blackpool.
> Scottish banner referring to the disastrous 1978
> campaign in Argentina.

●

So much pressure; 1966 was a garden party compared
to this. Nobody smiles!
> **Wilfried Gerhardt**, West German FA.

●

How sad to go out because you were too timid.
> **Ferenc Puskas** on England's performance against
> West Germany, a 0–0 draw.

●

It takes two teams to make a match. With respect,
I think there was a feeling in the German camp that
they were a little scared of us.
> **Ron Greenwood** after England's game with West
> Germany had been described as negative.

●

[Dino] Zoff's all right on the high stuff but with
low shots he's been going down in instalments.
> **Ian St John**, ITV Commentator, on Italy's veteran
> goalkeeper-captain who went on to lift the trophy.

●

This fellah [Marco] Tardelli, he's likely to leap out
of the TV at us. He's put more scar tissues on people
than the surgeons at Harefield Hospital.
> **Jimmy Greaves**, ITV pundit, on another of Italy's
> heroes.

●

Alcoholism v Communism.
> Banner at Scotland v Soviet Union game.

●

You are not at the seaside now, you know.
> **Billy Drennan**, Irish FA secretary, to the North-

46

ern Ireland squad who had dubbed their Madrid
hotel 'El Dumpo'.

●

They are a strange looking people. They wear Union
Jacks and tattoos, but some of them are really quite
nice.
>British Consul in Bilbao on England fans.

●

If we're going to die, we'll die with our boots on.
>**Cesar Menotti**, Argentina coach, on the eve of
>their vital match against Hungary. Argentina won
>4–1.

●

We are like the bull in a bullfight, who always
loses but in some ways, it wins.
>**John Adshead**, New Zealand football coach,
>surveying a World Cup group made up of Brazil,
>the Soviet Union and Scotland.

●

Italy surprised us by playing attacking football and
we failed to adjust to their unusual approach.
>**Cesar Menotti**, Argentina coach, after Italy's
>2–1 win.

●

Of course he should have sent me off, but that just
shows he had no authority. I told him he was whistling
for the Italians and he would have done better to have
put on a blue shirt from the beginning and swallowed
his whistle.
>**Uli Stielike**, West German defender, booked in
>the final by Brazilian referee Arnaldo Coelho.

●

This is not a dancing academy.
>**Claudio Gentile**, Italian defender, when accused
>of continually fouling Argentina's Diego Maradona.

●

This is not a good draw for England. It is not a

bad one, but certainly it is not a good one.

Sir Alf Ramsey, former manager, on England's grouping.

●

This is the most beautiful day of my life.

Dino Zoff, Italy's 40-year-old goalkeeper, holding up the World Cup.

●

If you're a Christian you can have one wife; if you're a Moslem you can have three; and if you're neither the sky's the limit.

Justin Fashanu, after meeting his long-lost father in Nigeria.

●

There have been more mistakes in the manager's office than on the field. Players we have bought have not lived up to their reputations; youngsters have been introduced to the side too quickly; we have sold two full-backs without replacing them – and so on. But I have not lost confidence in myself one iota.

Brian Clough on Nottingham Forest's mid-table placing.

●

You should never give the first kick but the adversary has to know that the second will be yours. In my career I got hit a lot, but I also left a lot of people by the wayside.

Pele, Brazil's legendary star, on violence in football.

●

Before long, clubs will be advertising for a commercial manager who is also qualified to coach.

Dave Bowen, Northampton Town secretary, on football's cash crisis.

●

I still think I could be the best vaulter in Britain, but I'm in danger of falling between two stools.

Brian Hooper.

Bowls is actually a young man's game which older people can also play at the same level.

Jack Hoskins, Australian champion, 58.

●

If you took me away from the golf tour, I'd be just another pretty face, but I'd like to see Bo Derek after 18 holes in 100 degree weather. Those cornrows and beads would be history.

Jan Stephenson, who is often compared with the film actress.

●

As for those new over-sized rackets, they're for women, old people and sissies.

Jimmy Connors at Wimbledon.

●

And in the Cup-Winners' Cup, Spurs will play either Eintracht or Frankfurt.

Alistair Burnett on *News at Ten*.

●

I'm one of a dying breed – a Chelsea season-ticket holder.

Dennis Waterman, TV actor.

●

There were more fouls than in any game I've ever played, but nobody except me seemed to think anything of it.

Trevor Francis, England footballer, after his first home match for Italian club Sampdoria.

●

I'd like to enjoy tennis. There are guys who play baseball who love baseball. That's not the way I feel. I've never loved tennis the way I should; the way people think I should.

John McEnroe.

●

I've lost contact with all my old friends. Sometimes I miss having other people to talk to.

Jayne Torvill, English ice dancer.

It upsets me to think of the millions paid for silly Picassos and other so-called works of art stored away in warehouses when the country seems willing to sacrifice the National, which undoubtedly is a work of art.

> **Ginger McCain**, trainer of three-time-Grand National winner Red Rum.

●

The question of South Africa has been the nigger in the woodpile.

> **Ken Turner**, Northamptonshire secretary, talking about the English cricketers' tour of South Africa.

●

In some respects soccer is a bit like the dinosaur. You give it a kick up the backside and three years later its head drops off.

> **Ron Jones**, Cardiff City managing director.

●

We were all outside waiting for blood to seep out under the door. It didn't, thank God.

> **Teddy Tinling** on the argument between John McEnroe and Steve Denton in the Wimbledon dressing-room.

●

I am a supreme optimist by nature and a pessimist by training.

> **Official Receiver** at Wolves.

●

Hold up a one-iron and walk. Even God can't hit a one-iron.

> **Lee Trevino**, American golfer once struck by lightning, advising others how to avoid a similar fate.

●

I had dinner with Mark on Saturday night and he told me my job was safe.

> **Ken Craggs**, 24 hours before being sacked as Charlton manager by chairman Mark Hulyer.

You English are all the same. You think the world waits for you.

Ralph Baumann, Swiss sailboard instructor, in a lakeside confrontation with Peter Coe and his son, Seb.

●

I think the title should go to the man who has the best total of finishes throughout the season. To finish first, first you have to finish.

Keke Rosberg, world champion racing driver, answering critics that he had won only one grand prix.

●

I'm finished with England. I'll never kick a ball for my country again. After ten years and 60 caps, I deserve better than to learn of my omission indirectly through the media.

Kevin Keegan after being left out by Bobby Robson.

●

When you've been thrown out of clubs like Barrow and Southport, you learn to live with disappointment.

Peter Withe on his omission from England's squad.

●

I've got a shelf full of trophies but most of them are for pigeon racing. It's about time I won a few for football.

David Hodgson, Middlesbrough player, before joining Liverpool.

●

Then there was that dark horse with the golden arm, Mudassar Nazar.

Trevor Bailey, BBC cricket summariser.

●

When you dream, as I did last night, that you've been picked to open the batting for MCC in Australia and come the great day you can't find your bat, you don't really need Freud or the Maudsley Hospital to give you

clues as to the balance in your mental account.
Jeffrey Bernard.

●

I was cheered, of course, by Mr May's phone call,
but at once I felt a deep sadness for Keith Fletcher.
Then immediately there was another call; it was from
the Gnome, deep in the Essex countryside; 'Good luck,
Goose, don't worry about me, I'll be alright.'
Bob Willis, England cricket captain.

●

Even among the horsey fraternity, I imagine viewers
are fairly cheesed off watching those same old riders,
Harvey Smith, Schockemole et al, going over the same
old fences on the same old horses night after night.
And not just this week, but all through the year. It
has become an advertising racket with a lot of people
doing very well out of it.
Richard Ingrams, editor of *Private Eye*.

●

He didn't intend to miss that one. Ninety-nine times
out of a thousand he would have potted it.
Ted Lowe, BBC snooker commentator.

●

In attaining his world record Mr Boycott has occupied
the creases of the world for 75 full days.
Bill Frindall, BBC cricket statistician.

●

I have given it much thought, and I'm not coming
to Wimbledon this year: I want to watch the World
Cup.
Jose Higueras, Spanish tennis player.

●

When I toured South Africa with Oxbridge Jazzhats,
I became physically ill after a week. We were being
used for propaganda. I will never return there.
Derek Pringle, Essex cricketer.

●

As for the darts team, it is not true to say there will
be no welcome for them – they are valued customers

I've been described as fat, boozy and toothless.
That's pretty accurate.
Jocky Wilson, Scottish darts player.

of many years standing. However, it is true to say that there will be no dartboard on the premises after the alterations.

Stockport Messenger.

●

There is no apartheid practised in South Africa's Grand Prix, because there are no coloured drivers or spectators.

Mike Reid, English motorcyclist.

●

Gerry Cooney [boxer] is understated, gentle, sensitive, understanding and real without momentarily compromising his macho.

Dennis Rappaport, Cooney's manager.

●

Being given chances and not taking them, that's what life is all about.

Ron Greenwood.

●

If you're up against a girl with big boobs, bring her to the net and make her hit backhand volleys. It's the hardest shot for the well endowed: like when I used to beat Ann Jones, she could hit under them or over them but never through them.

Billie Jean King, American tennis player.

●

People talk about the pressure in the game . . . Give me the pressure! Compared to the jobs I used to do, this is money for old rope.

Terry Griffiths, Welsh snooker player.

1983

We must be the only working-class family in Western Australia who have gone ex-directory.

> **Bill Donnison**, whose son Gary was the victim of a citizen's arrest which caused injury to the arresting Australian Test bowler Terry Alderman.

●

The main difference between rugby league and rugby union is that now I get my hangovers on Mondays instead of Sundays.

> **Tommy David**, Welsh forward who switched from union (played on Saturdays) to league (Sundays).

●

I think we can beat these blokes more often than not. They are a bit past it. I mean, poor old Lillee. He should have been out to grass long ago.

> **Robert Muldoon**, New Zealand prime minister.

●

There are some things about Ian Chappell I shouldn't have copied, like the way he always used to refuse to sign autographs in a bar. Here was me, 18, telling 50-year-olds to 'stuff off'.

> **David Hookes**, Australian Test batsman.

●

I realise it's a bad time to walk out on a job in football. But I have been putting in so little and taking out so much that if I hadn't resigned, I would have been taking money under false pretences.

> **John Bond** on leaving Manchester City.

●

My wife has been magic about it.

> **Bond** after news of his affair with a City employee broke 48 hours after he quit.

John Bond has blackened my name with his insin-
uations about the private lives of football managers.
Both my wives are upset about it.

> **Malcolm Allison**.

●

This surface is the best thing that ever happened
to English football.

> **Allison** on QPR's plastic Omniturf pitch after
> a 6–1 defeat there for his Middlesbrough team.

●

It seems that my team has been relegated from the
First Division while Jimmy Melia's team has reached
the Cup final.

> **Mike Bailey**, former Brighton manager.

●

If we go all the way to Wembley, it's difficult to
imagine the club looking elsewhere for a new manager.

> **Mike Bamber**, Brighton & Hove Albion chairman,
> on acting-manager Melia's job prospects in March.

●

We may have got to Wembley, but you have to
remember we've won only seven of 36 League matches
under Jimmy.

> **Brighton Director** on Melia's dismissal in Octo-
> ber.

●

How many more imaginary lets do you intend to
call, you fat turd?

> **John McEnroe** to a net-cord judge in Sydney.

●

If I had known I was going to be fined for what
I said, I'd really have let him have it.

> **McEnroe** after being ordered to pay 1,500 dollars
> for his outburst.

●

It's boring to play on clay again, you have to work
so hard for every point.

> **Mats Wilander** after five weeks on grass courts.

There's not a great deal wrong that half a season
of good results couldn't put right.
> **Frank McLintock**, captain of Arsenal's 1971–72
> Double team, on the 1983 side.

●

I've had to learn to shut my ears to all the insults.
I can't let these idiots think they're worrying me.
> **Alex Williams**, Manchester City's black goal-
> keeper.

●

Ask Nureyev to stop dancing, ask Sinatra to stop
singing, then you can ask me to stop playing tennis.
> **Billie Jean King** at Wimbledon.

●

I wouldn't want to play rugby – that's a very
dangerous game.
> **St Louis Cardinals** American football player at
> Wembley.

●

I'll start the car in the garage and run in there.
> **Alberto Salazar** on how he would prepare for
> possible smog during the Olympic marathon in
> Los Angeles.

●

I threw my racket to the ground and it took a weird
bounce of about 15 feet and went into the stands.
> **Hank Pfister** American tennis player, explaining
> why he received a warning during a match.

●

I was prepared to go on watching my weight, nine
o'clock to bed and not being able to have a drink with
my mates, but I'm not prepared to go on sacrificing my
family.
> **Pat Cowdell**, European featherweight champion,
> announcing his retirement from boxing.

●

It is very touching to see the loyalty of the fans,
but they are like the Red Indians . . . they are being

mopped up by civilisation and it's sad but inevitable.

Dr Desmond Morris, author and Oxford United
vice-chairman, as supporters demonstrated against
a proposed merger with Reading. The fans won.

●

Ballesteros is the No.1 . . . he hits the ball further
than I go on my holidays.

Lee Trevino.

●

They treat you as people, not footballers. If you have
a problem they'll sit down and talk to you about it.

John Devine, Norwich defender, on manager
Ken Brown and assistant Mel Machin.

●

You wouldn't expect a concert pianist to play with
a plastic piano.

John Prean, father of table tennis prodigy, Carl,
who was to boycott a tournament using plastic balls
instead of the traditional celluloid.

●

Compared to what is being made on the circuit,
the players are just pulling in nothing, or next to
nothing.

Martina Navratilova, winner of more than five
million dollars, talking about prize money in tennis.

●

As long as the test doesn't show up Phyllosan, I'll
be in the clear.

Peter Wheeler, England rugby union captain,
when he heard that players in the match against
the All Blacks were to be dope-tested.

●

If you all clap, perhaps many hands will make light
work.

West Ham announcer's loudspeaker plea during
a floodlight failure.

●

We've all been blessed with God-given talents. Mine

just happens to be beatin' people up.

Sugar Ray Leonard, boxer, before his short-lived retirement.

●

We had to watch an old lady being hurt by Leeds fans who punched her, and some of the fans even got into the corridor of the executive boxes.

Derby businessman complaining about the behaviour of Leeds fans.

●

Gordon made all three goals against Manchester City, but I left him out the following match as I wanted consistency from him and wasn't getting it while we were still down at the bottom of the league.

Jimmy Melia, Brighton manager, on why he dropped Gordon Smith.

●

The Jockey Club have issued a writ against the Texan who introduced Cabbage Patch dolls. They claim they have been making them for years – and calling them stewards.

John Francome, jump jockey.

●

Finding space was never a problem for me in the Western Desert during the last war and as for negative and positive play I thought that was something for the club electrician.

Bob Paisley, former Liverpool manager, on football jargon.

●

I was denied my place in history. I have a chance again to be bigger than life.

Sugar Ray Leonard explaining his return to the ring.

●

Just because I'm a professional it doesn't mean to say I'm not a human being.

Mick Mills, Southampton footballer, upset at

abuse from Sunderland fans because he did not
join the Roker club.

●

With his enthusiasm, I like to think he will stay
in the game, although he is an intelligent lad.

Ron Atkinson, Manchester United manager,
after Steve Coppell had been forced by injury to
retire.

●

I've been at Tottenham five minutes and I've already
been out for seven weeks.

Danny Thomas on his injury-troubled start at
Tottenham.

●

I've worked this fellow out now.

Tony Sibson after two rounds of his fight with
Marvin Hagler, who won in the sixth.

●

He can have the match ball instead of a rise. After
all, it's worth £30. We'll buy it back for £5 if he wants.

John McGovern, Bolton manager, after Tony
Caldwell had scored five against Walsall.

●

It's very difficult to play a guy who's hitting as hard
as he can and not missing anything and all the balls
are going in, and he's hitting the lines and the corners
all the time.

Ivan Lendl, Czech tennis player, sympathising
with the men he beat on the way to the US
Masters title.

●

The guy played almost incredibly. He always had
me off balance. He was all over me.

John McEnroe after his Masters defeat by Lendl.

●

You're bad, really bad. You're about as bad as I
am today.

McEnroe to a linesman during the same match.

He scares me.
Andrea Jaeger on John McEnroe.

It's been a slow process for me. I haven't been one of those 16 year olds winning the big ones. I like to keep a low profile. That's my image.

Jo Durie returning to tennis after injury.

●

I've no regrets. Without being big-headed, I think I've set football alight.

Ernie Clay, Fulham FC chairman, who had poured nearly £1.5 million into the club.

●

I had a call from Manchester City manager John Bond, my old boss at Norwich. Everything seemed in favour of my rejoining him. But I prayed about it all and afterwards had the unmistakable feeling that God didn't want me to go.

Justin Fashanu resolving a transfer dilemma.

●

The way everyone plays football now, the man will soon be moving faster than the ball.

Juan Lozano, leaving Anderlecht for Real Madrid.

●

If Sibson wins, he'll go home a national hero. If I win, I'll just go home.

Marvin Hagler. Hagler won.

●

Sure, I know where the press room is – I just look for where they throw the dog meat.

Nancy Lieberman, friend of Martina Navratilova.

●

What would I do if I won £1 million? Play five forwards.

Ron Atkinson, Manchester United manager.

●

At this rate they'll soon suspend me for having been kicked.

Diego Maradona of Barcelona after the Spanish FA had reduced – for a second time – their 18-match ban on Andoni Goicoechea, the 'Butcher of Bilbao'.

It can be very difficult to play doubles with your spouse. Emotional. Since there are no feelings, emotions between Jimmy and I, I'm sure we'll make a great team.

Chris Evert, joining former fiance Jimmy Connors for the world mixed doubles championship.

●

I was cheering and applauding for Trey Waltke, and only at appropriate times and not when John was serving. McEnroe said to me 'Are you going to cheer for my opponent all afternoon?' and I said: 'I'm working on it.'

Tennis fan suing McEnroe for allegedly throwing sawdust in his face during the US Open.

●

It's all a pack of lies. Anyway, how could you expect to bribe an entire team with just £40,000?

Ivanoe Fraizzoli, president of Inter Milan, when told of bribery accusations made by Dutch club Groningen.

●

I have to get away. People are waiting for me to get hit. They're waiting to see me put down. I need a break from the pressure.

Frank Bruno after his twentieth consecutive win.

●

We pass each other on the A52 going to work most days of the week. But if his car broke down and I saw him thumbing a lift, I wouldn't pick him up – I'd run him over.

Brian Clough on his former partner, Peter Taylor.

●

There is a rat in the camp trying to throw a spanner in the works.

Chris Cattlin, Brighton manager.

●

I'll put my money where my mouth is and bet anyone we stay in the First Division.

Graham Hawkins, Wolves manager, in August.

They were relegated at the end of the season, and in both of the next two seasons.

●

Players these days are highly paid. In fact, they get more than I do. They've got to face up to their responsibilities and start earning that cash.

Peter Hill-Wood, Arsenal chairman, after the Milk Cup exit against Walsall.

●

I've got the best safety game around but I don't like to use it because it bores me to tears.

Alex Higgins, Irish snooker player.

●

I remember looking at the clock and realising that about 15 minutes had gone and I'd hardly touched the ball. The next time I looked at the clock it had just gone twenty past three and I'd scored three times.

Mo Johnston of Watford after the 5–0 win at Wolves.

●

Allied Properties, owners of Wolves, have made this town the laughing stock of the country and have failed to invest in the team. This is the worst team I can remember.

John Bird, leader of Wolverhampton Council.

●

I know I am going to dislike him a lot. There are times when I'm going to smash rackets and get angry.

John Lloyd, English tennis player, joining Australian coach Bob Brett.

●

He is a classic case of a man needing someone to push him into pushing himself.

Bob Brett on Lloyd.

●

They've always had a lot of talent, a lot of good players . . . but they're like women. You know, they're all scratching each other's eyes out and wanting to do this, wanting to do that and I think that that has always been their downfall, as a team . . . as a great nation.

Ian Botham on Pakistan's cricketers.

●

What punch, Harry?

Frank Bruno to BBC's Harry Carpenter after American Jumbo Cummings nearly knocked him out in the first round.

●

Our methods are so easy, sometimes players don't understand them at first.

Joe Fagan, Liverpool manager.

●

I want to sell rugby league to the local people. The match-ball for our first game will be brought to the pitch by parachute. We also plan to have majorettes and Morris dancers. After all, this is Kent.

Paul Faires, chairman of the short-lived Maidstone club, Kent Invicta.

●

Agents do nothing for the good of football. I'd like to see them lined up against a wall and machine-gunned.

Graham Taylor, Watford manager.

●

We looked bright all week in training, but the problem with football is that Saturday always comes along.

Keith Burkinshaw, Tottenham Hotspur manager.

●

I was wrong to sign for Mr Clough . . . We rarely see the manager during the week, but we can find him in the papers every day.

Frans Thijssen, Dutch footballer, after leaving Ipswich for Nottingham Forest.

●

They came for warfare, to cause trouble and to fight. It has been said they are a small minority. They are not – there were 1700 of them and they were nearly all at it.

> **Bert Millichip**, Football Association chairman, on England football fans in Luxembourg.

●

On the [rugby union] club circuit in England and Wales there are roughly a dozen players I'd describe as psychopathic thugs. I don't think that's going over the top. In the context of what happened to me, that description isn't too strong.

> **John Davidson**, Moseley forward, forced to quit after his jaw and cheekbone were broken by a Swansea player.

●

Everyone knows Duran has been the dirtiest fighter around for years. That's what he does best, and that's what makes him so dangerous.

> **Marvin Hagler**, American boxer.

●

Hagler uses his bald head as a third hand. I'm a far cleaner fighter. He should be grateful I'm making him so much money. He would not get 10 million bucks for fighting anybody else.

> **Roberto Duran** of Panama.

●

When I took over Jocky [Wilson] in February he was sinking too much vodka and Coca-cola. I cut him from 12 to 3 a night. Now he can hit a playing-card side-on.

> **Mel Coombes**, darts manager.

●

I have hate for anyone who makes me leave my wife and baby. I might kiss him afterwards, but I'll tear his head off first.

> **Charlie Magri**, British boxer, before defeat by Frank Cedeno.

●

In terms of a 15-round boxing match we're not getting past the first round. The tempo is quicker. Teams will pinch your dinner from under your noses.

They don't give you a chance to play. If you don't heed
the warnings you get nailed to the cross.
> **Gordon Milne**, Leicester City manager, confused
> by football's First Division.

●

These are two marvellous New Yorkers, but they
talk funny.
> **Ed Koch**, Mayor of New York, on NY Marathon
> winners Rod Dixon (New Zealand) and Grete Waitz
> (Norway).

●

There's no way an amateur with 10 fights can beat
me. This kid should be sucking a bottle.
> **Larry Holmes**, US heavyweight boxer, before
> beating Marvis Frazier in round one.

●

I didn't run well, but then it was the first day
of my period.
> **Mary Purcell**, first woman home in the Dublin
> Marathon.

●

I reckon I sent two fans to hospital at the end of the
England-New Zealand game at The Oval. I worked on
a dockside for 30 years and I know how to dish it out
if I need to.
> **Don Oslear**, Test-match umpire, after brandishing
> a stump at pitch-invaders at Old Trafford.

●

The politics involved make me nostalgic for the Middle
East.
> **Henry Kissinger**, former US foreign secretary,
> after football's world governing body spurned his
> country's bid to stage the World Cup.

●

These kids don't go to parties, they don't socialise.
Everyone is concerned about practising, playing tennis,
not talking to anybody. It's a business. Women's tennis

has become junior tennis as far as I'm concerned.

Rosie Casals, veteran American player, on the teenage 'phenoms'.

●

Roger Knight is a smashing bloke but he's no captain. I asked him if I could do some bowling again and all I got was two balls when the other team needed two to win.

David Smith, Surrey cricketer, on leaving the club.

●

I find it ironic that Brian Clough should call for a total ban [on televised football] after making the kind of money as a member of TV's World Cup panel that would seem like a Pools win to most clubs.

Derek Dougan, ex-Northern Ireland centre-forward and TV panel pundit himself.

●

My only problem seems to be the Italian breakfasts. No matter how much money you've got you can't seem to get any Rice Crispies.

Luther Blissett on his transfer from Watford to Milan.

●

Looking back, some of the pictures I've posed for have been daft.

Charlie Nicholas, Arsenal and Scotland footballer and underwear model.

●

The conditions were very hot. I asked one of the lads after the match how he felt. I won't repeat what he said but it begins with N.

Alex Murphy, rugby league coach and commentator, after Salford v Wigan match.

●

I apologised afterwards to [Graham] Roberts. He's a hard man himself and understands these things. I'm sure he'll get his own back over the next five years.

Andy Gray, Everton striker, after injuring Spurs defender Roberts.

•

Rugby can be a very violent game if there is £1,000 per man riding on the result.

Bob Weighill, secretary of the Rugby Football Union, on the proposed setting up of a professional rugby 'circus'.

•

I don't know of another club in history who finished bottom of the league, sacked its star player [Geoffrey Boycott] and left the manager [Ray Illingworth] intact. The Yorkshire committee are guilty of the biggest whitewash I can ever recall.

Brian Clough, Yorkshire supporter and Nottingham Forest manager.

•

The decision [to sack Boycott] had to be made – it should have been made 10 years ago.

Fred Trueman, former Yorkshire and England bowler.

•

I've been swamped by letters from ordinary Yorkshire members who cannot contain their outrage. I've heard from others whose children won't stop crying because they will never see Geoff bat again at Headingley or Scarborough.

Sid Fielden, Barnsley policeman and pro-Boycott campaigner.

•

The greatest tragedy of his troubled life is that, above all, in the desire to be admired and loved by everyone, he has this enormous capacity for upsetting people.

Tony Greig, Boycott's former England captain.

1984

I do think even housing benefits are put into
perspective on occasions like this.

> **Rhodes Boyson MP** (Conservative), in House of
> Commons after news of Torvill and Dean's skating
> gold in Sarajevo Winter Olympics.

●

It was unfortunate Steve made so many mistakes
– our mother wanted us to tie.

> **Phil Mahre**, US special slalom skiing gold
> medallist, on his twin's second place in Sarajevo.

●

We had one netminder who couldn't stop a beachball
in a breeze, and one guy who could skate like the wind
but never took the puck with him.

> **Rod McNair**, Durham Wasps ice hockey coach,
> on two of his club's North American imports.

●

It was like trying to stop a train with a fishing rod.

> **Terry O'Dea**, darts player, on his 14-minute
> whitewash by Jocky Wilson.

●

An announcement will shortly be made after the
interim measures to be taken to undertake certain
of his duties pending discussions after any future staff
appointment.

> **Barnsley FC** announcement on managerial
> vacancy following sacking of Norman Hunter.

●

I'm in the electric chair now.

> **Bobby Collins** on succeeding Hunter.

The horse is a great leveller and anyone who is concerned about his dignity would be well advised to keep away from horses.

Duke of Edinburgh

●

Ray will find it rather strange joining us after all he has been through in recent years. He's joining a team where all the players actually talk and like each other.

Freddie Trueman welcoming sacked Yorkshire manager Ray Illingworth to the Old England charity-match cricket team.

●

It is bad enough that the *Daily Mail* has taken over the government of the country. It will be quite intolerable if they think they can take over sport as well.

Denis Howell, Labour's former Sports Minister, during the controversy over the granting of a British passport to South African-born Zola Budd.

●

In 1980 I was frightened to death of the competition. But I took it like a man, and came back.

Tessa Sanderson, Britain's gold medallist in the javelin at the Olympic Games in Los Angeles.

●

I'm looking forward to gloating over the performances of the US athletes.

Larry Ellis, US men's coach, before the Games.

●

Why runners make lousy communists. In a word, individuality. It's the one characteristic all runners, as different as they are, seem to share . . . Stick with it. Push yourself. Keep running. And you'll never lose that wonderful sense of individuality you now enjoy. Right, comrade?

Advert for running shoes in *Sports Illustrated* magazine, during the LA Games.

It was just as if they were a squad of trained paras – every one would die for one another.

David Whitaker, Britain's hockey coach, after team's bronze medal.

●

I'm tired of seeing my name in the same paragraph as Zola Budd.

Mary Decker before their collision in the Olympics.

●

It would be wonderful to be so pretty.

Zola Budd on Decker, whom she described as her 'idol', pre-Olympics.

●

Don't bother.

Mary Decker to Budd when the South African girl went to ask about her health after their clash which put the American out of the race.

●

What joy it has been to drive down streets and see American flags flying. The young athletes of the world have performed a miracle – they've brought back patriotism. Bless them all.

Letter to the *Los Angeles Times*.

●

The boycotts are not so terrible. There's no death involved. Olympics have survived massacres, cataclysms, destruction and 16 centuries of slumber. They are stronger than boycotts.

Monique Berlioux, Director of the International Olympic Committee, on the Eastern Bloc boycott of LA.

●

I'll be glad when they eliminate the word amateur from this sport.

Joe Douglas, Carl Lewis's business manager.

Reporter: What did Princess Anne say to you after you'd won, and who is going to be the mother of your kids?
Daley Thompson: Well you've just mentioned the lady. And the answer to the first question is 'I hope they'll be white'.

Press Conference exchange after Thompson's victory in the Olympic decathlon.

If Carl were to play pro football, he'd have to take a pay cut.

Joe Douglas after an unsuccessful approach from the Dallas Cowboys.

●

You can't train the way I do and go out with girls.

Joaquin Cruz, churchgoing Baptist, teetotaller and Brazilian gold medallist in the Olympic 800 metres.

●

I threw a hold and heard the Turk's elbow crack. I thought 'Oh no, they're going to disqualify me.' My brother didn't help when he broke some guy's knee off.

Mark Schulz, US wrestling gold medallist. Brother Dave was also in the team.

●

As long as an American is standing after three rounds it's hard to get a decision.

Redzep Redzepovski, Yugoslav boxer and silver medallist.

●

Out here I have been told by the manager where to go, where to stand and when to eat. I have hardly been allowed to make any decisions for myself.

Roy McGowan, Irish trap shooting champion, after finishing 53rd in the Olympic Games.

●

Everyone talks about how much money I can make but right now I don't care whether it's 50 cents or 50,000 dollars. I've got four gold medals and that's something no one can take away.

Carl Lewis.

●

I'd planned a loser's speech. I was going to say how happy I was with second or third. But I won. I love it.

Rowdy Gaines, swimmer, surprise winner of the 100 metres freestyle Gold Medal in the Olympics.

I shall be glad to get back to England and civilisation.
Peter Boden, unhappy with the organisation of
the shooting events in LA.

•

The Olympics make too many people nationalistic.
All that talk of brotherhood. Why, we've known
our competitors for years, meeting them in other
tournaments. And the anger and spite you saw in
our game today – it's hard to square that with the
Olympic ideals.
Richard Charlesworth, Australian hockey player
and Labor MP, in Los Angeles.

•

If the Russians had done half in Moscow what the
Americans did in LA everyone would have screamed.
In Moscow it was pretty fair play, but the Americans
were not fair play at all.
Monique Berlioux, International Olympic Com-
mittee director.

•

In a country like the USA, beauty is emphasised.
Superficial beauty, make-up. In the Eastern bloc, it's
just not a necessity for women to look like Mary Decker,
who looks like she goes two hours before the meet and
puts on make-up and curls her hair.
Ria Stalman, Dutch discus thrower.

•

No.1 is Jesus Christ because without his support
I wouldn't be here.
Carl Lewis, American multi-medallist at the
Olympic Games.

•

Remember, buddy, we're ABC Television. We bought
the Olympics. And we do what the hell we like.
US camera-crew man when advised that his
approach to Princess Anne was a breach of protocol
during the LA Olympics.

•

There is no way sport is so important that it can

be allowed to damage the rest of your life.

Steve Ovett.

●

One is always a little nervous when watching England bat.

Peter May, chairman of selectors.

●

When I went home from St Andrews I reminded the local mayor in Spain that he had promised to build a public nine-hole course after I won the US Masters. Instead of congratulating me on winning the Open he told the local newspaper I was a dummy, an idiot, a prima donna and that he made no such promise.

Seve Ballesteros.

●

It was lonely out there.

Bonnie Soms, only runner in the women's US Championship 10,000m.

●

I would like him to resign, but there's not an earthly chance of his doing so.

Sid Fielden, pro-Boycott leader in 1983, having changed his mind about Boycott's dual role as player and committee member.

●

To offer Geoffrey Boycott a new contract is akin to awarding Arthur Scargill the Queen's Award for Industry.

Letter to *The Yorkshire Post*.

●

I wouldn't play the French at marbles let alone rugby league. All we'll ever learn off them is how to fight and spit and bite each other.

Alex Murphy, former Wigan coach.

●

French Barbarians (a tautology if ever there was one) . . .

Simon Barnes, *Times* sports columnist.

He offered a completely new image of the French
rugby player, that of the sportsman.
> *L'Equipe*, French sports paper, on Jean-Pierre
> Rives.

●

This year? I never set goals but I want to improve
as a player, try to enjoy the sport and stay healthy.
And I haven't made any major resolutions apart from
being a wonderful guy on court.
> **John McEnroe**'s January view of 1984.

●

He was right on the three occasions he overruled
in my favour and wrong the time he did it against
me.
> **McEnroe**'s after-match verdict on British umpire
> Rob Jenkins.

●

Before I turned pro I didn't realise there was so much
money in the world. The amount is unreal, but I can't
just throw it in the garbage can.
> **McEnroe**.

●

It's me that's getting the hassle here. People even
ask me what colour toilet tissue I use.
> **McEnroe** at Wimbledon, after Ivan Lendl com-
> plained about 'Superbrat' being praised for his
> behaviour.

●

I don't know that my behaviour has improved all that
much with age. They just found somebody worse.
> **Jimmy Connors**.

●

He argued several calls which were seven inches out
and he said 'It was right on the line.' Maybe there's
something wrong with his eyes.
> **Jimmy Arias** after losing to McEnroe in France.

●

Shut your fat Frog mouths!
> **McEnroe** to President's box at Paris.

John's so good. Against him, all you can do is shake hands and take a shower.

Thomas Smid, yet another McEnroe victim.

●

If I don't win a trophy soon, I'll have to go to a shop and buy one.

Seve Ballesteros, before winning the Open golf at St Andrews.

●

Well, it's St Andrews isn't it? You know that every great golfer there has ever been has stood there and played a tee shot. You've got about six acres to aim at. You can make of it what you like. But that's a round of golf – a completely clean sheet before you start.

Freb Boobyer, veteran, on why he felt obliged to join the Open qualifying.

●

Craig Stadler came walking up and apologised to her. Then when he saw the watch was shattered he said 'Charge it to the R and A.'

Father of 12-year-old Alix Tindall, who was struck on the wrist by American golfer Stadler's drive at the Open.

●

I honestly cannot give my wife Denise any more excuses why I cannot quit.

Roger Jenkins, powerboat driver, announcing his retirement after the death of his friend and rival Tom Percival.

●

I've got a face made for radio.

Ron Luciano, American baseball umpire, on his failure as NBC-TV summariser.

●

New Yorkers love it when you spill your guts out there [Flushing Meadow]. Spill your guts at Wimbledon and they make you stop and clean it up.

Jimmy Connors.

78

I'm not the only one in the jockey's room who is sick of him. Lots of them are but they daren't say much. When he takes their rides they just shrug their shoulders and say: 'That's Lester.'

Darrell McHargue, American jockey, not joining the Piggott fan club.

●

I'm sick of that bloke's luck. He played well for two frames, but after that he was trampling in muck. I'll bury him next time.

Alex Higgins after a 5–1 snooker defeat by Steve Davis.

●

There must be an end to all this frustrating pushing the ball backwards and forwards by fat-cat professionals with Cartier chains around their necks, sunglasses in their tailored silk-shirt pockets and Porsches in the stadium car park.

Franz Beckenbauer, national team manager, on the state of football in West Germany.

●

I always remember after a dull Cup Final at Wembley, I was escorting the Queen to her car and I said: 'Did you think anyone played well today, ma'am?' and she said: 'Yes, the band.'

Sir Stanley Rous, reminiscing about his days as FA secretary.

●

Getting to the FA Cup Final caused the players and myself problems. A few of them got the bit about being stars. They want to make themselves pretty. I feel like taking the mirrors down from the dressing-room wall.

Graham Taylor, Watford manager.

●

I was more apprehensive about playing Wigan over two legs in the Milk Cup this season than I was against Porto.

Bobby Roberts, manager of Wrexham, after

his team had knocked the Portuguese out of
the Cup-Winners' Cup.

●

Women are flocking to gyms to train. They are seeing
pictures of women athletes on television – women with
no fat, tight bums and firm calves and they say 'Ah, I
like that.'

Carolyn Cheshire, British body builder.

●

It depends on who Jane is.

Steve Lundquist, US swimmer, questioned on
the likelihood of his becoming a film Tarzan.

●

Without being unkind, a donkey could lead the West
Indies at the moment. But put Clive Lloyd in charge
of Australia and even he'd struggle.

Keith Fletcher, former England cricket captain,
after Kim Hughes's resignation from Australian
captaincy.

●

I wish they would feed me some of the bums they
hand out to those boys. Every time I step into the
ring I face a war.

Pat Cowdell, British super-featherweight boxer,
on Frank Bruno and Erroll Christie.

●

It is the nature of the brain that separates man from
the lower animals. Boxing seeks to return us to the
level of lower animals. . . . People point out that rugby
is dangerous, that National Hunt racing is dangerous.
They are perfectly right. But the aim of these sports is
not to cause injury.

Dr Peter Harvey, a consultant neurologist.

●

I'm going to Russia to fight Gerrie Coetzee for $20
million.

Muhammad Ali, a retired fighter but a wishful
thinker.

I don't enjoy the way British teams play. When I came here three years ago, everyone was trying to win games by kicking rather than by scoring tries. Things haven't changed.

Mark Ella, Australian rugby union international fly-half.

●

I told them 'I'm glad I didn't have you four defending me when I had my court case. The judge would have put his black cap on.'

Tommy Docherty on his Wolves defence as the team continued its slide from First to Fourth Division.

●

I had a bash at positive thinking, yoga, transcendental meditation, even hypnosis. They only screwed me up, so now I'm back to my normal game plan. A couple of lagers.

Leighton Rees, Welsh darts player.

●

When there's a hosepipe ban covering half the country, you don't expect a damp wicket at Lord's.

Bob Willis, Warwickshire captain, on a wet end to his team's Benson & Hedges Cup final hopes.

●

This is a Test match. Its not Old Reptonians versus Lymeswold, one off the mark and jolly good show.

David Gower, England cricket captain, declining to criticise Malcolm Marshall's barrage of bouncers in fifth Test.

●

I've been looking up your cuttings. It's a fatter file than Adolf Hitler's.

American sports writer to Malcolm Allison.

●

I'm not excusing anything. But I was sick last night, sick a couple of times during the round and nearly fell

I always have to drink six pints before I'm
able to start playing properly.
   Bill Werbeniuk, 20-stone Canadian
snooker player, who claimed to consume
30 pints of lager a day.

over while standing over my put on No. nine.

Greg Norman beaten in the play-off of the Western Open.

●

If you want to win football games, you've got to score goals.

Graham Taylor, Watford manager.

●

The team performance was so poor I will not accept my wages this week.

Chris Cattlin, Brighton manager, after a 0–0 draw against Barnsley.

●

I never cease to amaze myself. I say this humbly.

Don King, boxing promoter.

●

They should show the kids films of his matches. They'd learn more from five minutes of George than they would from five years of coaching videos.

Pat Jennings, Arsenal goalkeeper, on George Best.

●

Graham Taylor and myself are going to pump nitrogen into the ball to make it go higher. Then we are going to give it a sedative at 2.30 p.m., an aspirin at half-time and paracetamol at quarter to five. After the match we are going to put the ball in a van and take it to a home provided by the national society for the prevention of cruelty to footballs.

Howard Wilkinson, Sheffield Wednesday manager, previewing the match with Watford, another club with a reputation for by-passing midfield.

●

Quick guys get tired. Big guys don't shrink.

Marv Harshman, in *Sports Illustrated*, on selecting basketball teams.

●

I want them to show disciplined aggression and obviously that will mean a few names taken by referees. In fact, if some of them don't get booked I'll be asking a few questions because it will mean they haven't got in their tackles.

Len Ashurst, Sunderland manager.

●

This looks a good team on paper. Let's see how it looks on grass.

Nigel Melville, new England rugby union captain, before the 19–3 defeat by Australia.

●

I didn't know what was going on at the start in the swirling wind. The flags were all pointing in different directions and I thought the Irish had starched them just to fool us.

Mike Watkins, Wales rugby union captain, after his first match at Lansdowne Road.

●

I must be the first winning captain to come straight into the dressing room and say 'We wuz robbed'.

Mike Watkins after Wales' win in Dublin, after which they found a thief had been at work.

●

All we can hope for is something to happen – probably rain.

David Gower, England cricket captain, during the West Indies' 5–0 'Blackwash'.

●

If snooker had not existed, TV would surely have had to invent it.

Geoffrey Nicholson, *Observer* journalist.

●

If Wales went to war with Russia tomorrow, I honestly believe Wales would have a bloody good chance.

Andrew Slack, Wallabies captain, before Wales-Australia rugby union international.

●

No leadership, no ideas. Not even enough imagination

to thump someone in the line-out when the ref wasn't looking.

J.P.R. Williams, former Wales captain, on the Welsh performance during the 28–9 defeat by Australia.

●

I'm grateful for what I've got, but I'm a clumsy git really.

Tony Sibson, British boxer.

●

I'm married with two boys, two girls and a tie-breaker on the way.

Jeff Jordan, American boxer.

●

I played 10 injury-free years between the ages of 12 and 22. Then suddenly it seemed I was allergic to the 20th century.

Nigel Melville, England rugby union captain, after spate of injuries.

●

I take the Gucci view about hard work on the practice field. Long after you've forgotten the price, the quality remains.

Alan Jones, Australian rugby union coach, on how rigorous training helped achieve a Grand Slam.

●

There is only me and the manager who have a laugh around here at the moment. Everybody is so damn serious. The only time they act daft is between three o'clock and twenty to five on a Saturday.

Kevin Morris, Swindon Town FC physiotherapist.

●

When I'm 38 or 40 I'd like to think I'm still bumming around tracks, doing it just for the sake of doing it. A lot of people will be saying 'God, he's still here. We all thought he was going to pack up and become a film star, but he's still bumming around the tracks, still

When I'm 38 or 40 I'd like to think I'm still bumming around tracks, doing it just for the sake of doing it. A lot of people will be saying 'God, he's still here. We all thought he was going to pack up and become a film star, but he's still bumming around the tracks, still being a pain.' That's what I want people to say.

Daley Thompson looking ahead.

●

You can make every effort to get a match played under difficult conditions, but a lot of people won't turn up to sit on ice or snow covered seats to watch it.

Alan Bennett, Leicester City secretary.

●

In this race, you don't ski alone, fear skis with you.

Steven Podborski of Canada on the eve of the super giant slalom at Garmisch.

●

The situation is a smaller version of the United States and Russia. They have their differences but they still have to live on the same planet. We have to realise that we have to live on the planet too.

Michael Crawford, Yorkshire chairman, on the county's interminable cricket war.

●

I don't think I can be expected to take seriously any game which takes less than three days to reach its conclusion.

Tom Stoppard, playwright-cricket fan, on baseball.

●

The neighbours, in their £80,000 terraced houses, who caused so much disruption at first, can go back to enjoying their Sunday afternoons in peace.

Brian Dalton, Fulham rugby league director, announcing the demise of the London club – soon re-born elsewhere.

I slept like a baby – every two hours I woke up crying.
> **Tom McVie**, New Jersey Devils ice hockey coach,
> after defeat by Buffalo Sabrres.

●

All fighters are prostitutes and all promoters are pimps.
> **Larry Holmes**, US heavyweight boxer.

●

Tommy Docherty criticising Charlie Nicholas is like
Bernard Manning telling Jimmy Tarbuck to clean up
his act.
> **Gordon Taylor**, secretary of the Professional
> Footballers' Association.

●

Charlie Nicholas? Seems like he's getting a lot of
everything except for the ball.
> **Jimmy Greaves**, ITV summariser.

●

On a boys' night out after a game the most I'll have
is seven or eight pints of lager. That to me isn't being
drunk.
> **Charlie Nicholas**.

●

On Mondays, which I set aside for developing skills
and positional play, there were sometimes only four
or five players turning up. From the others I'd get
excuses like 'My wife was having a tupperware party.'
> **Geoff Wraith**, resigning as coach to Wakefield
> Trinity rugby league team.

●

We went to Oporto and there's a bloody hurricane.
We come to Rome and the shops are shut. When we
play in the Soviet Union, Reagan will have probably
blown the place up.
> **Jim Steel**, Wrexham striker, during Welsh club's
> European Cup-Winners' Cup run.

It's difficult to play against a man . . . I mean against Martina. She scares you with her muscles.

Hana Mandlikova at the French Open tennis.

●

I bet my house she couldn't beat the 100th-ranked male player, and two she couldn't beat Harold Solomon.

Vitas Gerulaitas on Martina.

●

Even the men over 40 could beat us. My brother still beats me and he isn't ranked.

Chris Evert.

●

It's not that my concentration is bad but that I forget what I'm concentrating on.

Virginia Wade, English tennis player.

●

For two weeks I've been seeing the ball like a basketball, and today I couldn't see it.

Jimmy Connors, after losing 6–1, 6–1, 6–2 to McEnroe at Wimbledon.

●

I didn't think I deserved to get banned for so long, but it certainly taught me a lesson. I haven't been in trouble since then, apart from one little hiccup when I got sent off against Exeter last season.

Gareth Chilcott, England rugby union player, on the effect of his 12-month suspension for stamping.

●

What we do is none of their business. They just come to see us play.

Jerry Anderson, golfer, on the fans who report players for breaching the rules.

●

If those artificial pitches had stayed down they would have given a tremendous fillip to the development of similar pitches at grass roots level.

Freddie Brown, National Cricket Association president, regretting the removal of certain synthetic pitches.

I'm sure that if we could get a few more runs and hold our catches it would make a lot of difference, psychologically.

Allan Border, Australian captain, working out how to beat the West Indies.

●

When I was left out for the Milk Cup tie at QPR I told the manager I was embarrassed at learning about it in front of the other players. He said he had been embarrassed watching me play.

Paul Rideout asking to leave Aston Villa.

●

The only thing I wish is that when I come back on this earth I will be born lucky, instead of talented.

Bobby Campbell, Portsmouth manager, after the injury-time 1–0 defeat by Southampton.

●

A shrieking, whistling, fire-cracking mass of bias.

David Lacey, *Guardian* football correspondent, writing about Roma fans.

●

Reporters are trained to get things out of dummies like me, just as you are, sir.

Brian Clough giving evidence at an industrial tribunal.

●

People wondered how I would adjust. But Old Trafford folk drink tea and eat fish suppers as well you know. Why people should think it's all champagne and caviar beats me.

Lou Macari, moving from Manchester United to become Swindon manager.

●

I've an invitation from Mr [Ken] Bates for lunch, but it could turn out I'll have egg on my face if Chelsea don't go through with the deal.

Gordon Davies in the throes of moving from Fulham.

He is like a lot of people who know a job. They think they know a little bit more than they do.
>   **Brian Clough** on Malcolm Allison.

●

The hardest drug anyone would have taken would have been valium and that would have been on sleepless nights.
>   **Ian Botham** as the allegations of drug-taking on tour began to appear.

●

Kirk almost put me to sleep. The next time I play him I'm going to bring a bed. It was disgusting.
>   **Tony Knowles** after losing a snooker quarter-final to Kirk Stevens.

●

Athletes who become idols of the crowd when they are young can be swept away by the temptation of substituting their real personalities for those brief moments of glory.
>   **Pope John Paul**.

●

In top-class sport, you're the rooster one day, just a feather duster the next.
>   **Alan Jones**, coach of the Australian rugby union tourists.

●

When I arrived in the summer, one of my predecessors told the Spanish media that Meester Terry would be gone by Christmas. He forgot to say which year.
>   **Terry Venables**, Barcelona football club manager.

●

Boxing's supposed to be this heavy Mafia number, but if that's the case how come I've never been shot?
>   **Frank Warren**, London-based manager and promoter, who was to be gunned down in 1989.

●

It's very embarrassing – and we invented the game.
>   **Jon Mapley**, unsuccessful UK challenger for the World Tiddlywinks Championship.

Our rugby has gone bloody soft. In my day we wore our cuts and bruises and our cauliflower ears like war medals. You look at today's players and you can't tell whether they play prop or ping-pong. There's not a mark on 'em.

Ray Prosser, Pontypool rugby union coach.

●

I thought it was 19–0 . . . I must've lost count.

Alex Smith, Stirling Albion manager, after 20–0 Scottish Cup win over Selkirk.

1985

I don't care if he's George Best or Pele. Unless he's willing to do hard training he won't get a look in.
> **Malcolm Holman**, manager of the football team at Ford Open Prison, when Best was imprisoned there on a drinks charge.

●

We're expecting a lot of heavy praying.
> **Archie Phillips**, Hereford director, on borrowing church pews to accommodate the crowd for the third round tie with Arsenal. Arsenal won 7–2, after a replay.

●

My final wish is to be treated and accepted as any other British athlete.
> **Zola Budd** in January.

●

Can you imagine the genes Wayne (Gretzky) and I could put together?
> **Martina Navratilova** on her desire to have a baby by the Canadian ice hockey star.

●

I'm amused and flattered, but just not available for the job.
> **Wayne Gretzky**.

●

The safest place for spectators? Probably on the fairway.
> **Joe Garagiola**, US TV commentator, on celebrity golf tournaments.

I'd like to apologise to one person in particular –
the man who won the name-the-team contest and
got a ticket for life.

>**Paul Martha**, Pittsburg Maulers' President on the
>American football club's demise after one season.

●

I persuaded them that to take a towel out to Viv
Richards or to dry Clive Lloyd's socks is as good as
scoring 20 or 30.

>**Senator Wesley Hall**, West Indian team man-
>ager, on his tactics for keeping the young players
>happy when not playing during the 1984–5 tour of
>Australia.

●

One of our sprinters was told: 'You've got no chance
against me today, I've had an extra two pints from
the milkman.'

>**Jim Hendry**, British Olympic cycling team
>manager, claiming that blood-doping by American
>competitors had been prevalent in the 1984 Olym-
>pics.

●

Dutch goalkeepers are protected to a ridiculous extent.
The only time they are in danger of physical contact is
when they go into a red light district.

>**Brian Clough**, who signed van Breukelen and
>Segers from The Netherlands.

●

The best team always wins. The rest is only gossip.

>**Jimmy Sirrel**, Notts County manager, after
>being asked whether his side deserved to win
>at Huddersfield.

●

God has a task for each of us, and you just have to
do the best you can at it. For me, right now, it just
happens to be running a marathon backwards.

>**Albert Freese**, World Backwards Marathon record
>holder.

He is a very great Cricketer, but I wish
I had never met him.
Sid Fielden on Boycott as the Yorkshire
rebels began to fall apart.

Now I could die and it would be alright.

> **Libby Riddles** after winning the Alaskan Initarod trial sled dog race in 18 days, 20 minutes and 17 seconds.

●

It costs £20 for a pair of protective shorts, but if you don't have any you just jolly well get on the ice and get on with it.

> **Clare Platt**, Oxford University Women's ice hockey team.

●

Women's influence on the school sports system has wrecked it. They went for music and movement. Women are basically anti-competition.

> **Peter Lawson**, general secretary of the Central Council for Physical Recreation.

●

I'm still chasing the birds but now I'm catching them.

> **Sports Council slogan** persuading young people to take part in sport.

●

They let you chase girls. They just don't let you catch them.

> **Glen Kozlowski**, Brigham Young University American Football captain on going to a Mormon University.

●

We're the mean machine, the bovver birds. The meaner you are the better. You make more money that way. You get remembered.

> **Lolita Loren**, woman wrestler.

●

What it boils down to is this: when are you a woman and when are you a man? It's gotten out of hand.

> **Wayne Demilia**, a spokesman for the International Federation of Body Building, on the increasing use of anabolic steroids.

A lot of beautiful girls may be made available to you before the game. Such traps are aimed at destabilising you. You are going to war, and must be on the lookout for all kinds of weapons.

King Mtetwa, Swaziland home affairs minister, to Highlanders FC players before an Africa Cup match in Lesotho.

●

A woman's place is at home with her babies. There would be a lot less trouble in the world if women stayed at home.

Eddie Thomas, manager of boxer Colin Jones, objecting to the appointment of a woman judge for his world title fight with Don Curry.

●

I'm an ordinary person. I like the taprooms of this world. That's where people are genuine. Other people control them, employ them and run their lifestyles, but they are the backbone of the country.

John Lowe, darts player.

●

Not only do I want to be president of the Rugby Football Union in 1994, but also I am a truly wonderful person and books like this don't make much money.

Andy Ripley, on why profits from *Ripley's Rugby Rubbish* were being given to charity.

●

I'll have to ask my sergeant for time off.

Wade Dooley, 6ft 8in policeman and rugby union forward, on his selection for England.

●

It didn't demoralise us, but it moralised them.

Dick Greenwood, England coach, and the mistake which cost a try early in the defeat by Wales.

His style is more suited to rugby union.
> **Udo Lattek**, Bayern Munich coach, on Andy Gray after Everton's European Cup Winners Cup semi-final victory.

●

He's Ireland's No.1.
> **Liverpool Kop** greeting Manchester United goalkeeper Gary Bailey after his error had given Ireland a goal against England at Wembley.

●

If you think champagne, you drink champagne. At Sunderland they think water.
> **Ian Atkins**, former Sunderland captain, then at Everton.

●

I just opened the trophy cabinet. Two Japanese Prisoners of War came out.
> **Tommy Docherty**, Wolves manager, on the club's dire position.

●

We don't use a stop watch to judge our golden goal competition. We use a calendar.
> **Tommy Docherty** as his side went two months without scoring.

●

If you gave our strikers a £50 note they'd find it difficult to score in a brothel.
> **Tommy Docherty** again.

●

It's a bit like joining the Titanic in mid-voyage.
> **Rachel Heyhoe-Flint** on being appointed public relations officer of Wolves in April.

●

After the match an official asked for two of my players to take a dope test. I offered him the referee.
> **Tommy Docherty** after Wolves' 5–1 defeat by Brighton had confirmed their second successive relegation.

You can stop counting – I'm not getting up.
> **Jim Watt**, former world lightheavyweight champion's suggestion for his tombstone epitaph.

●

Wrestling is showbusiness. Boxing is fighting.
> **Frank Warren**, boxing promoter, when Prince Charles's secretary declined invitation to the Jones v Curry fight by saying that HRH could not attend 'the wrestling match'.

●

You Grunt, I'll Groan.
> **Jackie Pallo** autobiography title. Book alleged matches were fixed.

●

Never had a ball. Oranges. All the time, oranges.
> **Kenneth Achampong**, Fulham's African-born forward, on how he acquired his ball control.

●

I've spent six years watching that bastard Walker and then he goes and scores two goals against us.
> **John Leftley**, Chelsea fan arrested for trying to punch Sunderland's left winger.

●

This particular scum must be driven out of the seats and back on the terraces where they can more easily be monitored and controlled.
> **Ken Bates**, Chelsea chairman.

●

What comes next – water cannon, guards, tanks and consultant undertakers to ferry away the dead?
> **Simon Turney**, Greater London Council public services committee, on Chelsea's proposal to put up an electric fence in front of the Shed.

●

If people did not have the filthy, dirty habit of smoking, there would be 56 people alive today.
> **Stafford Heginbotham**, Bradford City chairman, after the Valley Parade fire disaster.

These were fire matters and not my responsibility.

John Laird, the Government Health and Safety Executive inspector, on his failure to take action over the fire risk at Bradford City.

●

The pressure on schools is to be anti-competitive. PE teachers are positively discouraged from the job they were trained to do.

Paul Chapin, PE teacher, resigning in protest at ILEA policy on school sport.

●

The whole competitive ethic is becoming unfashionable. It's a terrible loss. I believe that playing team sport is a great formative experience.

Peter Lawson, CCPR.

●

It looks as though your side is a bit younger these days. No, it's just that we now all tackle.

Exchange between Trevor Brooking and his ex-manager John Lyall after West Ham had beaten QPR.

●

All I could see was the ball. I thought I had a 50–50 chance of getting it.

Kevin Moran, Manchester United defender, on the tackle that led to his becoming the first player sent off in an FA Cup final.

●

Fifteen years for that? You get better trophies playing pool.

Joe Farrag, Everton supporter, on the Canon League trophy which replaced the old Football League championship one.

●

We used to think Liverpool were cocky when they talked about the derby as just another game. We'd be discussing it for weeks beforehand. But now we know what they meant.

Kevin Ratcliffe, Everton captain, as his team challenged for the treble.

●

I have played football since I was a toddler. Left wing, as you would expect. I was very fast.

Robert Maxwell, millionaire publisher, ex-Labour MP and chairman of Oxford United.

●

He stole the glory from the players and spoiled a night which should have been for the players and the supporters.

Jim Smith, former Oxford manager, on the night Maxwell turned the club's promotion celebrations into what some claimed was a propaganda campaign against the local council.

●

If somebody is celebrating, it means we still have much to learn.

Giorgio Cardetti, Mayor of Turin, after Juventus' European Cup Final win over Liverpool in the aftermath of the fighting which cost 39 lives at Heysel Stadium.

●

Where are we going? What the hell are we doing? Why the hell do these people keep paying me?

Alkis Panagoulas, US national soccer coach, on his country's footballing state before the match with England, who won 5–0.

●

Comprehensives do not produce cricketers.

Jim Laker, former England bowler.

●

I'm going to make them wear their caps this season. You don't award a player his county floppy hat, do you?

Jack Bond, Lancashire cricket manager.

It should be a cause of real concern to cricket administrators that the batsman himself has become as much a target for the fast bowlers of the world as the wicket he defends.

   Wisden editorial.

   ●

If you have guys who are going to stay around and be stubborn, and obviously make fast bowlers look like they are not fast bowlers, I can't see why they shouldn't be softened up a bit.

   Viv Richards, West Indies captain, replying to *Wisden*'s criticism of Marshall's bowling to Pocock the previous summer.

   ●

I'm upset, annoyed, disappointed, fed up, to say the very least.

   Phil Edmonds, England spinner, on being omitted from the first Test v Australia.

   ●

I can't understand why a bloke can't put his foot down behind the line.

   Allan Border, Australian captain, on his bowlers' problems with no-balls.

   ●

What goes on in the middle is our business. It's nothing to do with you.

   Mervyn Kitchen, umpire, replying to press questioning about the no-balling of Jeff Thomson during the Australians' match with Essex. Thomson bowled 26 no-balls.

   ●

You see the highlights. I see the failures. For motivation purposes the failures are more important to me.

   Tim Robinson, England opening batsman, after his 175 in the first Test v Australia.

We are fitter than any side I have ever known at Yorkshire.

David Bairstow, Yorkshire captain, after preseason training at Catterick Army camp.

●

NEW BALL PAIR No.14

Yorkshire Post headline as the county's seam bowlers struggled with injuries.

●

It was a bit like trying to take an up-and-under with a pack of angry forwards bearing down on you.

Allan Border on Geoff Lawson's attempt to take a catch as the crowd poured onto the field at the end of the Headingley Test.

●

At Headingley, before play on the Saturday of the first Test, I heard one Yorkshireman mutter, none too affectionately, 'here comes t'clown', as the blond-dyed hulk stepped out of his car wearing black leather trousers and a deck-chair blazer. Later that day in the dressing-room he paraded his thigh-length cowboy boots before me. Between the two fashion shows he struck a magnificent 60.

Mike Brearley on Ian Botham.

●

Gower not only has to prove that he is worth a place as captain but also as a batsman at Lord's.

Fred Trueman before the second Test. Gower went on to make 732 runs in the series.

●

Botham couldn't bowl a hoop downhill.

Fred Trueman. Botham took 31 wickets in the series.

●

A few gentlemen, some professionals, a couple you'd rather not introduce to your mother and at least one you'd cross Oxford Street to avoid.

Frances Edmonds on her husband's England colleagues.

He looked like a dying dingo when he went to court.
>**John Feaver**, Cumberland Club director on Peter
>Johnston, the Australian tennis player who left
>£1,000 in a taxi.

●

I am not prepared to practise eight hours a day
or go on a diet just to be No.1
>**Mats Wilander**, Swedish tennis player, before
>Wimbledon.

●

It's hysterical. The committee only had one decision
to make and they chickened out.
>**Pam Shriver**, American tennis player, on the deci-
>sion to seed Chris Evert and Martina Navratilova
>as joint No.1s at Wimbledon.

●

Chris and my mother both belong to the club of No.1.
But I think Chris would be better in No.10 than my
mother would be on the other side of the net.
>**Carol Thatcher**, daughter of Margaret and
>biographer of Chris Evert.

●

The average guy has a pathetic body and when
they see me they feel threatened.
>**Martina Navratilova**'s explanation for her un-
>popularity with male spectators.

●

I didn't want to cause anybody to spill their straw-
berries and cream. But I think I showed a lot of
guts.
>**Anne White**, American tennis player, on appear-
>ing at Wimbledon in white alabaster body stocking.

●

I don't care who you are trying to protect. No one
comes in here without a pass.
>**Wimbledon steward** refusing entry to Frank
>Sinatra's 18-strong bodyguard.

She needs a haircut. And those calves are
bigger than mine.
   Martina Navratilova coming face to face
with her model in Madame Tussauds.

I don't want to sit in that box at that wonderful place and risk the embarrassment of seeing an American disgrace our country.

Charlton Heston turning down a seat in the Royal Box because of John McEnroe.

●

If you guys could get just one per cent of the stories right!

John McEnroe to the Press.

●

You guys put certain players on the plateau up there. But there are a lot of other good players around and today I just proved once again that we fellows exist.

Kevin Curren, South African player, to the press after beating McEnroe at Wimbledon.

●

I can't wait to not have to play Wimbledon again.

McEnroe after his defeat.

●

He's got the balls, and when he's holding them he controls the tempo.

Jimmy Connors after defeat by Curren.

●

I didn't have a watch contract when I was 17. He is like a marketing thing already. When I was 18 I acted 18. He doesn't seem to act his age.

McEnroe on the new Wimbledon champion, Boris Becker of West Germany.

●

Ten years ago I would have said it was questionable whether a Christian joining the tennis circuit could have prospered spiritually and grown in his faith. Based on what has happened in the last two years, I would say that there is light on the tennis court, and that there is an opportunity for someone to incorporate Christian living and tennis.

Sandy Mayer, American tennis player.

Being a Christian I cannot imagine a missionary saying 'We won't go there until apartheid is finished.'
    Alan Knott on a 'rebel' tour to South Africa.

●

An example of the Lord's guidance came for me with my decision to join [Kerry] Packer's World Series Cricket.
    Alan Knott, ex-England wicketkeeper, in his autobiography *It's Knott Cricket*.

●

Watching Roebuck was like being at a requiem mass.
    Jim Laker, BBC cricket pundit. Roebuck had criticised Laker's commentary.

●

Phil Edmonds needs two more field changes to get his 1,000 for the season.
    Jim Laker

●

One viewer told me the other day that listening to my old mate Jim Laker and his new sidekick Bob Willis was better than taking two Mogadon.
    Fred Trueman

●

I just hope people won't think I'm a swine and a rotter.
    J.R.T. Barclay, Sussex captain, after declaring Sussex's innings with Gehan Mendis four short of a record fifth century in six innings. Mendis left at the end of the year.

●

I thought things were changing with people like Gatting and Botham leading their counties. But Hampshire obviously still prefer public schoolboys. Perhaps I don't have enough initials – it is a handicap having only two.
    Trevor (T.E.) Jesty on leaving Hampshire after being passed over for the captaincy in favour of M.C.J. Nicholas.

I really needed to get into a race where I would
be pushed.

> **Mary Slaney (Decker)** after just beating Kirsty
> McDermott.

●

There was so much barging and shoving it was like
trying to get into a Glasgow pub on a Saturday night.

> **Tom McKean** on the European 800m final, which
> he won.

●

Of course I'm strong. I'm an Englishman.

> **Lester Piggott** after a narrow victory in a hectic
> finish to the French 1,000 Guineas.

●

I went through a stage of feeling awful to one of
feeling terrible. Once I started to feel terrible I was
OK.

> **Steve Ovett** after the California Mile in San
> Francisco.

●

I don't watch television myself but my family do,
and they tell me that the most popular programmes
are the ones which are full of violence. On that basis
football ought to do rather well.

> **Jack Dunnett**, chairman of the Football League,
> on the faltering TV negotiations less than a month
> after the Brussels disaster.

●

We are opposed to FIFA's over-reaction. One even
wonders whether it is political.

> **Peter Robinson**, Liverpool chief executive, on
> the brief worldwide ban on English clubs in the
> wake of Brussels.

●

The politicians, the police and Uncle Tom Cobley and
all lay the blame for hooliganism squarely on football
clubs. Even their own governing body appeared to
wilt under the pressure when it fined impecunious
Millwall £7,500 for an attack on the police by a crowd

of hooligans at Luton, some 40 miles or so from their ground. Where is the justice in this? How can Millwall FC possibly be held responsible? The yobs, of course, got off scot-free and lived to fight another day.

George Cubitt, deputy chairman of the CCPR.

●

I hope she is not going to be two-faced enough to turn up in the royal box at the next cup final, because she hasn't been football's friend.

Brian Clough on the Government response to
Bradford and Brussels.

●

Because of the weather I think there will not be
a very good champion this year.

Seve Ballesteros during the Open, won by British
golfer Sandy Lyle.

●

He's the best bloke in the world to caddy for. My wages must be the best on the tour, and when I stay at his house at Wentworth he brings me tea in the morning. Just tiptoes in, milk and no sugar.

Dave Musgrove, Lyle's caddy.

●

I adore the game of golf. I won't ever retire, I'll play until I die. Then I want them to roll me into a bunker and cover me with sand. And make sure nobody's ball lands in there for a while.

Lee Trevino.

●

I am convinced they will not want to race. They have been brought up with love and security. They will not need to prove their superiority to their friends; they will not be complex characters in that way.

Nikki Lauda on his children's future after his
own retirement from motor racing.

●

I am sure that young people learn more about social behaviour through sport and recreation than they do in any classroom. Organised games in particular teach

108

self-control, the value of unselfish co-operation, the importance of abiding by the rules of the game and the ability to take success and failure calmly and philosophically. This is clearly illustrated in the contract between the behaviour of most players and the behaviour of so many spectators.

Duke of Edinburgh.

●

THATCHER'S BATTING FOR THE ASHES ... OF DEMOCRACY IN LAMBETH.
HAWKE DOESN'T GIVE A XXXX FOR ABORIGINAL LAND RIGHTS.

Banners at the Oval Test.

●

The West Indies must be quaking in their boots.

David Gower, England captain, after England's 3–1 victory in the Ashes.

●

It's going to be very hard to convince people that we really do have a lot of very promising young players.

Allan Border, Australian captain, anticipating a frosty reception at home after the Ashes defeat.

●

I think they must be mad!

Phil Edmonds on being made 12th man by Middlesex – the day after he had helped England win the Ashes.

●

If I could bowl at myself I'd be very keen. It'd be an amputation job to get the ball out of my hand.

Kevin Jarvis, Kent seam bowler, whose batting average then was 3.15, after preventing Jonathan Agnew from taking all 10 wickets for Leicestershire against Kent.

●

It seems there is one rule for Botham and one for the rest.

Yorkshire committeeman after Botham had been reprimanded for dissent and Bairstow had received a suspended four-match ban for a similar offence.

●

Ignorant, biased, bigoted and a bunch of racial idiots.

Ian Botham on the Headingley crowd after the alleged taunting of Viv Richards.

●

Yorkshire followers are very tolerant of ethnic communities. We shall be delighted when the first coloured player arrives in the team.

Reg Kirk, Yorkshire chairman.

●

In Italy we don't have good net facilities.

Alfonso Jajarayah, captain of the Italian cricket touring team.

●

I don't like that Hubert H. Humphrey Metrodome. It's a shame a great guy like Humphrey had to be named after it.

Billy Martin, New York Yankees manager, on the Minneapolis baseball stadium.

●

I told him not to be such a great big baby.

Stan Seymour, Newcastle United chairman, on Jack Charlton's decision to resign after being jeered by the crowd.

●

If there was a vacancy, Barry could become President of Ireland tomorrow if he wanted.

Donal Creed, Irish minister for Sport, after McGuigan's world championship win over Eusebio Pedroza.

●

Silly lies and bunkum.

Harold Larwood, former England bowler, on the television drama series *Bodyline*.

●

Nowadays I serve and then I rush to the net. Usually the ball beats me and just rarely I manage to hit it.

Either way the point ends there, so I can get a breather.
Jean Borotra, still playing tennis at 87.

●

I've been through a list of all the players who have been mentioned, and I've got a hell of a team.
ABC commentator on the players named in the baseball drugs scandal.

●

If no other lesson emerges from the agonising confessions in Pittsburgh, athletes now know that you can't trust a pala with a straw up his nose.
Chicago columnist on the players' readiness to shop their team-mates in the drugs trial.

●

I can't remember the last time I didn't spend $300 or so a day on coke.
Kirk Stevens, snooker player, confessing cocaine addiction.

●

I hate the city, the environment, Flushing Meadow. They should drop an A-Bomb on the place.
Kevin Curren after his defeat in the US Open Championships in New York.

●

He should get down on his hands and knees and thank God he's here, not in South Africa.
Ed Koch, Mayor of New York. Curren, a US citizen, was born in South Africa.

●

It was nice to stand in the winner's circle and not to have to share 50 per cent of the money with my brother.
Tom Gullikson, doubles specialist, on winning his first singles title for 11 years.

●

He turned it down because they couldn't guarantee any hills for the players to run up and down.
Mike Lyons, Sheffield Wednesday defender, ex-

plaining why his club's manager Howard Wilkinson refused a job in Saudi Arabia.

●

He has done enough damage without letting him walk off with our equipment. If he wants to give us £40 he can have it.

Alan Durban, Cardiff City manager, refusing to give Trevor Senior the match-ball after Senior's hat-trick for Reading.

●

Sport is cut and dried. You always know when you succeed. Even when you are 12–0 down in a 25-frame match you are in with a chance, but when you have lost it is finished. You are not an actor; you don't wonder 'did my performance go down all right?' You've lost.

Steve Davis, British snooker player.

●

Kenny Dalglish would have made the perfect trade union official.

Graeme Souness, Liverpool team-mate.

●

There is black and white proof that I'm not the killer I'm supposed to be. I've only been sent off twice.

Graeme Souness.

●

They like me in Japan. I'm small, yet I can hit the ball 300 yards.

Bernhard Langer, the US Masters Champion, on his $60,000 Japanese clothing contract.

●

If the crowds back in America ever got like this, I'd never hit another golf ball.

Hal Sutton having trouble with spectators at The Belfry during the Ryder Cup.

●

I bet Sutton can't wait to get back to America today and head straight for a MacDonalds.

Tony Jacklin, European captain.

I looked at my wife and said 'Honey, our guys are getting a spanking out there.'
Lee Trevino, US captain on the Ryder Cup defeat.

●

The order to make it all-ticket came from No.10, so at least Mrs Thatcher's advisers should come and see what a right muck-up they've made.
Ernie Clay, Fulham chairman, on poor ticket sales for the match v Leeds.

●

We're talking about a woman who has probably never been to a match in her life as a fee-paying person, giving advice to everyone on how they should run matches. She destroys everything else that is important to working class people, so why not football as well?
Derek Hatton, Liverpool councillor, Militant leader and Everton fan.

●

I hope Mrs Thatcher was watching!
Gary Lineker after scoring a hat-trick v Turkey. Earlier in the summer his £800,000 transfer fee had been heavily criticised by the Government.

●

Brazilians are too expensive and the French are unavailable.
Egyptian FA spokesman on the unpopular appointment of ex-Hull and Wales manager Mike Smith as national coach.

●

The mesmeric effect of flickering flames can cure a bad patch by helping players rehearse moves in their minds.
John Syer, sports psychologist and Spurs adviser.

●

I think all our players have got central heating.
Peter Shreeve, Spurs manager.

It is very difficult to practise your serve when the earth is moving.

> **Henrik Sundstrom**, Swedish tennis player, on playing a Davis Cup match in Chile after an earthquake.

●

The Bratislava girls are employing man-to-man defence.

> BBC basketball commentator.

●

I don't care if West Ham don't get mentioned in any national newspaper.

> **John Lyall**, manager.

●

You go to other people's grounds, you run 'em. It's just enjoyment all the time. Like a tennis player gets all geared up to play, we get all geared up to fight. Tribal, innit? Football is one tribe onto another. We fight cos we like fighting.

> West Ham's 'Inter City Firm' member in TV documentary *Hooligan*.

●

Ian represents everything that's best in Britain. He's Biggles, the VC, El Alamein, the tank commander. He's everything. I mean, how could a schoolboy not want to be like Ian Botham.

> **Tim Hudson**, Botham's agent.

●

He is to appear alongside Oliver Reed as a murderer and a rapist . . . he can't wait to get cracking.

> *The Sun* on Ian Botham's supposed move to Hollywood. It never came off.

●

The British Athletic Board believes it is non-racist, yet it is seriously undemocratic. Blacks are first-class citizens while they are winning, and second-class when they stop.

> **Ron Pickering**, athletics coach and BBC commentator, on the lack of black coaches and officials.

There was blood everywhere. I got it all over my coat. My wife and 12-year-old daughter had to leave, it was so sickening. It would have turned me into an anti-boxing guy if I'd seen it on TV.

Ferdinand Pacheco, once Muhammad Ali's doctor, now a commentator, explaining why he had advised NBC not to transmit the Kaylor-Walker bout.

●

My culture is not the culture of Ray Mancini. I want to destroy him and cut him up real bad. I want to ruin his face and flatten him out and forget him.

Livingstone Bramble before his bout with Mancini. He won.

●

I guess we burned our ships coming across here, but there was no longer any incentive to perform in South Africa . . . and sport is about incentive.

Rob Louw, Springbok rugby union player, on his and Roy Mordt's decision to sign for Wigan.

●

GOBBLEDEGOOCH

South African Newspaper headline after Gooch's statement on apartheid had eased the way for the 1986 tour of the West Indies.

●

You drop your shoulder and move round a defender only to discover he didn't read your first dummy. So you crash straight into him and he comes away with the ball.

Trevor Brooking on playing Sunday morning football for Havering NALGO.

●

Wait till we play them at The Valley.

Chris Cattlin, Brighton manager, after his side's 5–3 home defeat by Charlton. Charlton had left The Valley for Selhurst Park two weeks earlier.

You don't hear people singing 'You'll never walk alone' at Charlton home games too many times.

Lennie Lawrence, Charlton manager, several weeks after his club's move to Selhurst Park.

●

All-out attack mixed with caution.

Jim McLaughlin, Shamrock Rovers manager, on his tactics for a European Cup tie with Honved.

●

He'll never forgive Bob Geldof for thinking of Live Aid before him.

Midlands Journalist on Birmingham manager Ron Saunders' Save Our Society campaign.

●

Team spirit is an illusion you only glimpse when you win.

Steve Archibald, Barcelona striker.

●

It's going to be a draw between your teams, we know that. And for us four years of hard work will just vanish.

Mircea Lucescu, Romanian team manager, before the decisive England v Northern Ireland World Cup qualifying group match. He prophesied correctly.

●

Try telling Pat Jennings it was a fix.

Billy Bingham, Northern Ireland manager, after Jennings' magnificent save in the last minutes earned his team the draw at Wembley which took them to the World Cup finals.

●

Like you, during a long and tempestuous history, we came under the yoke of our Anglo-Saxon brothers. You, wisely, had more sense than us, in that you devoured as many as you could.

Alun Thomas, Welsh Rugby Union president, welcoming the Fijian tourists.

Newport have been branded an aggressive side, but the opposition came onto us. If we had joined in the free-for-all it would have been an all-out battle.

Mike Watkins, Newport captain, after their explosive match with Fiji.

●

I told them 'Fellows, I'm not prepared to condone this type of street violence.' Before going I told the players 'You obviously don't need me.'

George Crawford, rugby union referee who walked off 20 minutes into Bristol v Newport match.

●

We hope we'll be playing each other again on a regular basis. Time is a great healer. After all, we trade with Japan.

Alan Skeats, president of Richmond on his club's decision to resume fixtures with Llanelli six years after they were discontinued over a row over rough play.

●

What is needed to stamp out dirty play is leadership and authority. When I was a referee I never sent anyone off in 13 years. If there was any spiky business I would immediately show the players who was boss.

Denis Thatcher, consort to the Prime Minister.

●

I packed up smoking but couldn't relax. Now I'm smoking again – only 20 a day – and I've given up jogging and I'm much happier.

Terry Griffiths, snooker player.

●

Your first win is like making love. You enjoy it so much the first time that you want to do it again and again.

Nigel Mansell after victory in the South African Grand Prix soon after winning the British one.

Eating will now be an entirely new ball game. I might have to buy a new pair of trousers.

Lester Piggott on his retirement as a jockey.

●

I'm 35 fighting young men. Rocky Marciano was 25 and fighting old men. Rocky couldn't carry my jockstrap.

Larry Holmes to Peter Marciano, Rocky's brother, after losing to Spinks.

●

I don't understand how I can be paid to play for Kingston as an amateur, yet be classified as a professional for playing in a United States basketball league when I didn't sign a contract or accept any money.

Martin Clark on being ruled ineligible to play for England.

●

I'm sorry. I meant that I would like to run full-time and get paid for it.

Steve Anders, amending his statement that he would like to be a professional runner after a protest by the BAAB. His revised version was acceptable.

●

One word sums it up. Voluptuous.

Terry Marsh, Essex fireman and boxer, on winning the European Light-Welterweight title.

●

Being a celebrity is like rape.

John McEnroe.

●

I am not a scientist and I am not talking to brain surgeons.

Graham Lowe, New Zealand coach, on his rugby league tourists.

●

If Walt Disney had seen this little man's antics, there'd have been no Mickey Mouse.

Ray French BBC rugby league commentator,

This was the month when it was revealed that Zola Budd got £90,000 for running a race, then proved she was still an amateur by finishing fourth.

Two Cheers for November, BBC World Service programme.

on Hull scrum-half Peter Sterling.

●

It's not Terry Holmes that Bradford need – it's
Sherlock.

Alex Murphy, BBC pundit, on the latest league
recruit from union.

●

The players don't have to swallow a crumb of
Russian food if they so wish. We're travelling with a
full kitchen of Irish food – rashers, eggs, black puddings
. . . everything fresh and vacuum-packed. There can be
no excuses on that score.

FA of Ireland spokesman on the Republic's
preparations for the World Cup qualifying match
in the Soviet Union.

●

I was sad about making the decision to resign, but
I could not go on having the crowds of yobbos yelling
insults at me every time I walked down the tunnel.

Eoin Hand, Ireland manager, after the 2–1 defeat
in Moscow.

●

It's easy enough to get to Ireland. Just a straight
walk across the Irish Sea as far as I'm concerned.

Brian Clough confirming his interest in replacing
Hand.

●

There are men who fear women more than they
love cricket.

Geoff Scargill, seconding the motion to admit
women to full membership of Lancashire County
Cricket Club and hence to the Old Trafford
Pavilion. It failed to get the necessary two-thirds
majority.

●

Let them in, and the next thing you know the place
will be full of children.

Lancashire member opposing the motion.

Give us a pavilion behind the bowler's arm, put a
bar in it and the women can go where the hell they
like.

> Lancashire member putting cricket considerations
> first.

●

I won't let the men take any liberties. If there's
any dissent in indoor cricket the batsman can have
five runs deducted and if he keeps doing it he can be
ordered off. I won't be frightened to send them off.

> **Dawn Trowsdale** on becoming the first woman
> umpire at Lord's.

●

I know the musicians are boycotting it, but it's a bit
daft. South Africa is not as bad as everybody makes
it out to be.

> **Sandy Lyle**, British golfer, on playing in the
> $1 million Sun City Classic.

●

I've never been invited to black Africa anyway.

> **Lee Trevino** on being blacklisted by the UN
> for taking part in the same tournament.

●

I don't understand politics very well.

> **Sandy Lyle**.

●

They're not so different. They have two arms and
two legs, and some of them even have heads.

> **Frank Arok**, Australian manager, before the
> World Cup qualifying play-off match with Scotland.

●

It's every player's dream to turn out against Brazil
and tuck one of their shirts in the drawer.

> **Billy Hamilton**, Northern Ireland forward, when
> the 1986 World Cup draw put his team in Brazil's
> group.

●

Alan Cunningham has been a revelation to me. I
didn't realise how great a job he could do on and

off court. He's our best defensive player and our best offensive rebounder.

Danny Palmer, Portsmouth basketball coach, in his programme notes for the Prudential Cup semifinal. By the time the game arrived Cunningham had been released. Portsmouth lost.

●

I'm only a hamstring away from oblivion.

Steve Jones after winning the Americas Marathon.

●

The year of the hamstring.

Ron Atkinson, Manchester United manager, on a series of injuries.

1986

If we can sell Newcastle Brown to Japan, if Bob
Geldof can have us running round Hyde Park, and if
Wimbledon can make it to the First Division, there is
surely no achievement beyond our reach.
>   **The Prime Minister**, the Rt Hon Margaret
>   Thatcher.

●

We were very disappointed we couldn't play on
Saturday, because like United we had supporters
coming from all over the country. There were two
coming from London, one from Newcastle, one from
Brighton . . .
>   **David Kilpatrick**, Rochdale chairman, as his
>   side's FA Cup 3rd round tie with Manchester
>   United at Old Trafford was postponed.

●

You can only play this game one time. If they
[wives and girlfriends] can't wait, tell them to take
a cold shower.
>   **Mike Ditka**, Chicago Bears coach, announcing
>   a pre-Super Bowl curfew to his team.

●

American Football? Hell, what is it? It's a sick game –
a whole lot of guys trying to beat the crap out of one
another. If I could play golf just as well, I'd do it.
>   **Jim McMahon**, Chicago Bears quarterback.

●

To date not much is known of the Irish team, the
combined efforts of the ABA and George (We Import
More Paddies Every Year) Wimpey having failed to

extract the information which makes international
matches so much more interesting.

Sponsors' press release before an amateur boxing
international. Wimpey were the sponsors.

●

This government says it intends to drive hooliganism
out of sport – yet it appoints a hooligan to oversee it.

Richard Course, Executive Director of the League
Against Cruel Sports, on Minister of Sport, Dick
Tracey.

●

Some of the ravines are so deep that if you topple
over, your clothes will be out of date by the time you
hit bottom.

Tony Pond, driver, at the Monte Carlo Rally.

●

I hope the ban won't affect the sponsorship deal
I have with Ford.

David Coleman, TV commentator, on his drink-
driving ban.

●

Our forwards can do things the English forwards
cannot. We have hands.

Jacques Fouroux after France's 29–10 win in
Paris.

●

Save that for the dance tonight, lads.

Clive Norling, Welsh referee, to Lenihan (Ireland)
and Dooley (England) as they grappled at Twickenham.

●

Some of their players had big bellies, and one of
their defenders looked nearer 40 than 30.

Jim Hagan, Birmingham City defender, on the
Altrincham side which put the First Division team
out of the cup.

●

It was not the Liverpool we are used to seeing. I don't
know what they were trying to do, and I don't think

they knew either.

Kevin Ratcliffe, Everton captain, after scoring
in his side's 2–0 derby win at Anfield in February.
Three months later Liverpool had done the double.

●

Larry Holmes got $10 million against this guy and
we got $7.50 an hour.

Stanley Barowski, Pennsylvania security officer,
after helping to subdue boxer Gerry Cooney in a
bar brawl.

●

If that's a local derby, it's a good job we don't play
Rotherham.

Tom Morton, Doncaster official, after 5 players
had been sent off in the first 19 minutes of a rugby
league match against Sheffield Eagles.

●

When you have to spend the tour in your hotel room
so you are not stitched up, there's something wrong.

Ian Botham being pursued by the media during
the West Indies tour.

●

If a quarter of the things said about me were true,
I'd be pickled and I'd have sired half the children in
the world.

Botham.

●

My ghost is writing rubbish.

England cricketer during the West Indies tour.

●

There was a certain gentleman out there who managed
to find some practice facilities.

Ray Illingworth after England had replied to
criticism for not practising by saying that nets
weren't available. The 'gentleman' was Geoffrey
Boycott.

The net practice was voluntary.
>**David Gower**, England captain, explaining a poorly attended practice session.

●

If he ever tried refereeing in the US, he'd turn up in an oil drum at the bottom of the Miami River.
>**Art Ross**, Birmingham Bullets basketball coach, on an English referee.

●

Cricket civilises people and creates good gentlemen. I want everyone to play cricket in Zimbabwe. I want ours to be a nation of gentlemen.
>**President Mugabe**.

●

He looks like a cuddly little panda.
>**Tony Brown**, England manager on the West Indies tour, on Mike Gatting after the England batsman's nose was broken.

●

I have never felt it more likely that we should see someone killed.
>**John Woodcock**, *Times* Cricket Correspondent, on England's mauling by the West Indies pace attack.

●

If we had shown the kind of attitude and guts in the war that our cricketers have shown in the West Indies, Hitler would have walked all over us.
>**Brian Close**.

●

If you get six head balls an over, that's showbiz.
>**Phil Edmonds** after an assault by Patrick Patterson.

●

Sorry Gerrie, but that's cricket.
>**Frank Bruno** after beating Gerrie Coetzee in March.

It'd have had to be six baboons in there to beat
me tonight, Des.

Bruno to Des Lynam after the same fight.

●

Witherspoon was too much of a beast for Bruno.

Jim Watt, former World lightweight champion,
on Bruno's defeat in July.

●

It's no place for me here, I'd rather be at home
reading my bible.

Lynette Bruno, Frank's mother, at the ringside
for the Witherspoon fight.

●

I love children and I like discos, shopping and most
of the other things that appeal to girls of my age.
It's just that when I get into the ring, I'm a fighter
by instinct.

Lisa Howarth, Thai Kick Boxing World super-
flyweight champion.

●

We get all the fights and people sent off.

Joanne Lloyd, Streatham Strikers Women's Ice
Hockey team captain, insisting that the women's
game is as exciting as the men's.

●

If Fulham's first team showed as much skill on the
field as they did in bed, they would be in the First
Division.

Len Rosendale, Fulham FC driver, alleging that
his bus had been used for orgies.

●

I'd rather have a guy take me to a football match
and have a drink afterwards than go to bed with
someone.

Samantha Fox.

●

The fact is that I have, at various times in the
past, smoked pot.

Ian Botham admitting that a 1984 story about

his drug-taking was true in the face of allegations of harder substances during the West Indies tour.

●

I have been to many functions where some great cricketers of the past have been present. To see some of them sink their drink is to witness performances as awe inspiring as ever any of them displayed on the cricket field.

Ian Botham defending his use of marijuana.

●

Certainly I am told you can play cricket better after a marijuana cigarette than after a couple of pints of beer.

Lord Wigoder, Old Bailey judge and cricket follower.

●

I missed the last goal. I was too busy counting our share of the money.

Ken Bates, Chelsea chairman, after the much criticised Full Members Cup produced gate receipts of £508,000 at the Final.

●

It sounds like a campaign to blacken my name.

John Fashanu, Wimbledon forward, on Portsmouth complaints about his over-physical approach.

●

What do they expect me to do? Walk round in a T-shirt with 'I'm in Charge' on it?

David Gower responding to Peter May's doubts about his laid-back approach to captaincy.

●

QUEREMOS FRIJOLES, NO GOLES
(We want beans, not goals).

Mexican Steelworkers' banner at the World Cup opening ceremony.

The proof of the pudding is when you get down
to the nitty-gritty.
Billy Bingham, Northern Ireland manager.

●

What do you know about Portugal?
I went there for my holiday.
Exchange between **Brian Clough** and **Peter
Shilton** before the England v Portugal first round
match.

●

Briefly, Trev, do you think Beardsley should play?
Very briefly, Bri, I've never ever seen him play.
Exchange between **Brian Moore** and **Trevor
Francis**.

●

The Iraqis don't take any prisoners.
Ron Atkinson.

●

Anybody who knows the Irish knows that when we
are provoked sometimes we bite.
Billy Bingham after a bad-tempered draw with
Algeria, who were accused of spitting at their
opponents.

●

We had a Mauritian referee against Paraguay.
Mauritius is a lovely island, but they don't play
football.
Evaristo de Maceda, Iraq coach.

●

There was a murderer on the pitch today – the referee.
Omar Borras, Uruguay manager, on the Italian
official who sent off one of his players after 45
seconds against Scotland.

●

I may have a German passport, but I have a Danish
heart.
Sepp Piontek, Denmark's German coach, when
his team faced West Germany.

They call him the Salmon. Not because he leaps
in the air, but because he always ends up in the net.
> **Terry Venables** on Valdano after Argentina's
> centre-forward had missed an easy header and
> finished up in the net.

●

He gets great elevation on his balls.
> **David Pleat** on Maradona.

●

Conjugate the verb 'done great'. I done great. He
done great. We done great. They done great. The
boy Lineker done great.
> Letter to *The Guardian*.

●

Two Gary Stevens, there's only two Gary Stevens . . .
> England fans' song in Mexico.

●

I won't be going anywhere near the German goal
– no closer than 40 metres.
> **Patrick Battiston**, French defender, rejecting the
> idea of renewing close acquaintance with Harald
> Schumacher.

●

I wouldn't blame anyone for not turning up. I'm
sure the Almighty will understand.
> **Rev Dick Ackworth**, St Mary's Church, Taunton,
> anticipating a low attendance at evensong which
> clashed with England v Argentina.

●

A little bit the hand of God, a little the head of Diego.
> **Maradona** on his 'handled' goal which defeated
> England.

●

We blasted the English pirates with Maradona and a
little hand. He who robs a thief has a thousand years
of pardon.
> *Cronica*, Buenos Aires newspaper. The report was
> headed 'Malvinas 2 Ingleses 1'.

MARADONA, porque no naciste en Mexico?
>   Banner at the World Cup Final.

●

This German team produces defensive, working soccer.
If we win the cup it could be very bad for the future.
>   **Paul Breitner**, former West German captain,
>   before the 1986 Final.

●

This is a poor Argentine team.
>   **Cesar Menotti**, manager of the 1978 Argentina
>   World Championship team, on the 1986 side.

●

With Maradona even Arsenal would have won it.
>   **Bobby Robson**.

●

Diego sometimes disappeared from games in Mexico
for long periods. He was waiting for things to happen,
not making them. The next four years will really tell
us if he deserves to be called an all-time great. He still
has more to do to convince me.
>   **Pele**.

●

If our lot (Liverpool) had been out here, we'd have
done the treble.
>   **Jan Molby**, Denmark and Liverpool midfielder.

●

They moved very slowly from one side of the ground
to the other. They also complained about the sun's
reflection off parked cars. We are just not used to
these sort of tactics.
>   **Audrey Collins**, Women's Cricket Association,
>   after India had bowled only 8 overs in the
>   penultimate hour of the England v India match
>   at Harrogate.

●

The MCC should change their name to MCP.
>   **Diana Edulji**, Indian Women's touring team
>   captain, on being refused entry to the Lord's
>   pavilion during the men's Test.

Gin-soaked dodderers.

Botham's description of the selectors at a private
dinner in Manchester.

●

The easiest job I ever had. Ian told me when he
proposed to bowl – and when he was coming off.

Julian Wyatt, Somerset Second XI captain, on
finding Botham in his side after suspension.

●

There is very little common ground between me
and the average player. Frankly I think most famous
cricketers are too big to play county cricket.

Ian Botham to Peter Roebuck in 'It sort of Clicks'.

●

It's not an end to my ambition. I haven't played
for England a third time yet.

Geoffrey Boycott after scoring his 150th first
class century against Leicestershire in June.

●

I just bowled straight. It gave me a lot of pleasure,
but I can tell you I'm not available for the Australian
tour.

Ken Higgs on taking 5–22 against Yorkshire
in August, in his first game for Leicestershire
for four years at the age of 49.

●

IF YOU ALL HATE HARROW, CLAP YOUR HANDS!
Eton Boys at Lord's.

●

It was like batting against the World XI at one
end and Ilford Second XI at the other.

Anonymous England batsman on Hadlee and his
New Zealand colleagues' bowling in the Lord's Test.

●

Pavilion steps are the last place you expect to meet a
car. You get a few knocks playing cricket, but never
anything like this.

Paul Kingsbury, Endon batsman, after being

knocked over by a car driven by an opponent.
Kingsbury lost 3 pints of blood.

●

Not a good night for Zola Budd. She died on the
last lap and finished fourth.
IRN News report.

●

Dis game of tennis, she drop dead if McEnroe don't
come back soon.
Ion Tiriac, Becker's manager. McEnroe left the
circuit for a period after a spell of poor form.

●

I'll buy John McEnroe his ticket and hotel next year
so everyone can pick on him instead.
Ivan Lendl on taking over McEnroe's role as
the Wimbledon hate object.

●

Tennis has missed me, there's not much question of
that. I think tennis is boring. It was boring when I
was there as well, but I made it less boring.
McEnroe.

●

Somebody should teach you a lesson in respect.
John McEnroe to Boris Becker.

●

When Ivan Lendl was winning rounds at Wimbledon,
all papers described each success as another demon-
stration of the benefits of a vegetarian diet. But when
Boris Becker actually won, not one put it down to the
dietary benefits of Wurst.
Geoff Harrington, director of planning, Meat
and Livestock Commission.

●

The problems are all in his head. The trouble is
he's discovered a world outside tennis.
Dr Irving Glick, USTA, on McEnroe.

●

John has reached the stage where he no longer cares
what happens to him. He's like the boxer who gets hit

133

by a good punch and grins to acknowledge it.
John Newcombe on McEnroe.

●

My only interest outside boxing is making love.
Lloyd Honeyghan

●

I realise this may shock some people, but they all
get on very well together.
Mickey Duff, Honeyghan's manager, on revela-
tions that his fighter has four children by three
women.

●

All that's left for me to do is go find John Lloyd
and start a family.
Pam Shriver, American tennis player, after
first-round defeat at Wimbledon.

●

You cannot judge Lenny, or any other player, on
the basis of his last shot.
Rev Jesse Jackson, on Len Bias, Boston Celtics
basketball player, who died of cocaine intoxication
at 21.

●

If you think it's hard meeting new people, try picking
up the wrong golf ball.
Jack Lemmon, actor.

●

Golf is the most straight-forward, honest competition
in the world. There are no substitutes allowed, the
game doesn't require a lot of officials. In a goldfish
bowl it tests your physical and mental skills, your
patience and your perseverence. You play in all kinds
of conditions. You get lousy breaks and good breaks,
and you have to cope. It is almost life.
Deane Beman, Commissioner of the USPGA,
and occasional professional player.

This has been one brutal day for golf. Some of the
best players in the world have been humiliated out
there.

>   **Greg Norman**, the ultimate winner, on the first
>   day of the British Open in a gale at Turnberry.
>   •

It's not a common entrance exam, it's an honours
degree.

>   **Michael Bonallack**, Secretary of the Royal and
>   Ancient club, defending Turnberry.
>   •

If the players thought the rough here was bad, wait
until they see Muirfield next year.

>   **Alistair Low**, chairman of Turnberry, responding
>   to American players' criticisms.
>   •

Everyone owes tax, don't they?

>   **Lester Piggott** on being charged with tax evasion.
>   •

I've appointed Maurice Setters as my assistant. He's
well placed, living in Doncaster.

>   **Jack Charlton**, soon after becoming manager
>   of the Republic of Ireland.
>   •

I shall not be voting, nor can I influence the vote.
There are 90 members of the Olympic Committee, and
they are all independent.

>   **Juan Samaranch**, Spanish IOC chairman on the
>   race to host the 1992 Olympic Games. Barcelona
>   won comfortably.
>   •

It's a shambles. The only communication I've received
was a letter telling me to make my own way to the
Games.

>   **Steve Ovett** on the disorganisation leading up
>   to the Commonwealth Games in Edinburgh.

Their efforts have brought shame and embarrassment to Scotland.

The Scotsman editorial on the Commonwealth Games Organising Committee.

●

I don't want to have anything to do with Mrs Thatcher. These are not Mrs Thatcher's games, they are Edinburgh's games, Scotland's games, the Commonwealth's games. If I get a deficit, clearly she should look forward to receiving a bill from this organisation.

Robert Maxwell in his role as joint chairman of the Commonwealth Games Organising Committee.

●

A preposterous idea.

Robert Maxwell rebutting a report that in return for his financial contribution to the games he would present the winners' medals.

●

It would have been churlish to have refused the committee's kind invitation to play a part in the ceremony.

Maxwell two days later, after presenting the medals.

●

I have a love-hate relationship with him. I hate him when I'm in the water, but love him when I get out.

Sarah Hardcastle, Commonwealth Games double gold medal winner, on her coach Mike Higgs.

●

Unfortunately the gods weren't shining on the right person. I've waited two long years since LA. Two years for the gold medal in a championship. And now I'm humiliated.

Fatima Whitbread, javelin thrower, on being pipped by Tessa Sanderson's last throw at Edinburgh.

Give me a mended leg and a bottle of Grecian 2000
and I'll be as good as new.

Peter Reid on his long lay off with injuries in 1986.

●

For the benefit of Anglo-Saxon viewers, I wonder
if the TV sports presenters would consider using
subtitles when interviewing Kenny Dalglish.

Letter to the *Standard*.

●

Years ago school staff were willing to devote their
spare time to the game, and children were proud to
play for their school, but not any more. There is no
honour attached to the school game any more.

Robert Lynch, Secretary Liverpool Schools FA,
on the state of schools football.

●

We would be against competition during the school
day. If competition takes place in inter-school matches,
then that is an extra-curricular activity, and should be
taking place after 4 p.m. or on Saturday mornings.

Carole Rowbotham, ILEA senior PE instructor.

●

Some local education authorities actually think competitive sport is bad for children. They'll be telling us
next that water doesn't suit goldfish.

Dick Tracey, Minister for Sport.

●

Hundreds of sports grounds are being sold off to
developers secretly as there's no requirement to notify
the government. It is causing us serious concern that
many children are not getting the chance to play
football or cricket.

Nigel Hooks, CCPR technical officer, on local
councils' response to the government's encourage-
ment to dispose of surplus land.

It seems to us ironic that politicians are always quick to cash in on sporting success, but not so quick to lend financial support.

> **Arthur McAllister**, AAA chairman, on the government's decision to freeze the Sports Council's grant.

●

Hindsight is a wonderful thing, but it invariably comes too late.

> **Stafford Heginbotham**, Bradford City chairman, on Valley Parade fire recriminations.

●

Who writes your script?

> **Graham Gooch** to Ian Botham when Botham took a wicket with his first ball on recall to the Test side after his suspension.

●

I don't expect to have to pay for my racing.

> A Royal Yacht Squadron member hearing that Cowes Week had financial problems.

●

Ten per cent of the boats on the Solent never go beyond the Needles, but a large slice of those who matter in British industry are down there.

> **Brian Hulme**, chairman of Sandhurst Office Equipment, explaining why his firm sponsor Cowes week.

●

I may be black, but I know who my parents are.

> **Viv Richards**, jumping into the crowd at Weston to confront some racist hecklers.

●

The reason he's struggling to bowl straight is because his head's in the wrong place.

> **Fred Trueman** on Greg Thomas.

It wasn't so much the light that bothered me as
the pounding of my heart as the ball came down.
>   **Graeme Fowler**, Lancashire, on the catch which
>   ended Trevor Jesty's brilliant innings and took
>   Lancashire into the NatWest Trophy Final.

●

I've never seen any bugger get 300 in a day.
>   **Brian Close** on Ken Rutherford's innings of 317
>   at Scarborough.

●

In the eyes of the rugby union, having a game of
rugby league, whether amateur or professional, is like
introducing Aids to the dressing-room.
>   **Alex Murphy**, St Helens coach.

●

Rugby is a physical game and no place for the fair sex.
>   **John Jeavons-Fellows**, North Midlands rep on
>   the RFU, opposing a proposal to give a display of
>   women's rugby at Twickers.

●

You can kick for touch any day, but you only live once.
>   **Jonathan Davies**, Wales stand-off half, on his
>   adventurous approach.

●

You can't expect to fire cannons from a canoe.
>   **Tom McNab**, athletics coach, on the need for
>   England's rugby players to improve their training.

●

People say that because of a lady's shape, it isn't
possible for them to play snooker well. That shape
hasn't prevented Bill Werbeniuk earning a decent
living.
>   **Allison Fisher**, world ladies' snooker champion.

●

Cricket shouldn't be used as a political football.
>   **David Graveney**, Gloucestershire captain.

Like Maradona I too used my hand, but only to
pick my birdies out of the hole.
Vicente Fernandez, Argentina Golf Captain,
after beating England at St Andrews.

●

To bring clubs like Manchester United and Tottenham
to a ground like Wimbledon's is ridiculous.
Ted Croker, FA Secretary, advocating the abo-
lition of promotion and relegation.

●

I should think the only time he's been to Wimbledon
was to see the ladies tennis final.
Dave Bassett, Wimbledon manager, replying to
Croker.

●

I wrote to Dave Bassett thanking him for taking
Wimbledon into the First Division. I realized their
arrival would deflect a lot of the abuse from us.
Compared with them we're supposed to be cultured.
Howard Wilkinson, Sheffield Wednesday man-
ager.

●

I've heard the manager is going to give me a medal.
If I was a car, they'd have to turn the clock back.
Nigel Worthington, Sheffield Wednesday defender, on surviving 5 years of Wednesday's rigorous
training.

●

They'll all be dead by 26.
Nico Claesen, Spurs' Belgian international, en-
countering Wednesday for the first time.

●

All the matches won't be like this, will they?
Terry Butcher, Rangers, on his first Scottish
League match v Hibs. Eight players were booked
and Rangers' player-manager Graeme Souness
sent off.

If I had my way Celtic would make an immediate
application to join the English League.

> **David Hay**, Celtic manager, after his team had
> one player sent off, 7 booked and lost on a disputed
> penalty in the Skol Cup Final v Rangers.

●

Familiarity breeds aggravation.

> **Billy McNeill** on the effect of Scottish Premier
> League clubs playing one another four times a
> season.

●

I have refereed a lot of Scottish matches in my time,
but never one like this. Both teams went out not to
play football but to kick one another.

> **Alex Ponnet**, Belgian referee, after sending off
> two Rangers players in their UEFA Cup match
> v Borussia Moenchengladbach.

●

The days of hitting your opponent's balls into the
shrubbery are over.

> **Brian MacMillan**, Croquet Association Secretary.

●

My chap (caddie) says hit a quiet eight-iron and I
follow his instructions and, sure enough, it finishes
on the green. But how do you get that ball in the
hole here, I cannot find the answer.

> **Paul Tembo**, Zambian Dunhill Cup golfer at
> St Andrews.

●

You can't learn to play American football just by
watching Channel 4.

> **Jake R. Hilder III**, Texan coach to Glasgow Lions.

●

As far as I'm concerned, you are part of the buildings
and the furniture at Somerset and so are Vic and Ian
... I hope that you'll be able to play with us until
those legs turn to jelly, because I think that you and

I and Ian and Vic are Somerset players right down to our bootstraps.

Peter Roebuck's letter to Viv Richards on his appointment as Somerset captain for the 1986 season.

●

When you have two work horses and shoot them in the back I think it's evil. You don't treat animals in this way. I was blindfolded, led up an alley and assassinated.

Viv Richards on hearing in August that Somerset were not renewing his contract.

●

I don't take back a word of what I said. But over the season my feelings changed.

Roebuck in October.

●

Sacking Viv Richards is like sending Shergar to Argentina for dog meat.

Ian Botham.

●

This committee has done for fair play what Colonel Gadaffi has done for air safety.

Jan Foley, Bristol barrister, putting the Somerset rebels' case at the Somerset special general meeting, 1986.

●

We had great difficulty this summer in getting him (Richards) to play in our evening pub games – he declined to play at Clevedon, Truro and Braunton, and the only reason he played at Ottery St Mary was when we reminded him that they had staged a benefit match for him the year before.

Michael Hill, Somerset chairman, defending the committee decision.

I'm told that Peter Roebuck is flying out to have
a man-to-man talk with me. I suggest he stays in
London. He'll be a whole lot safer there.

> **Ian Botham** on hearing the confirmation of
> Somerset's decision to sack Richards and Garner
> while in Australia.

●

This race has turned round and bitten me in the
backside.

> **Nigel Mansell** after losing in Mexico.

●

It wouldn't surprise me if the Welsh Selectors arranged
a fixture between all the Williamses and Joneses.

> Welsh rugby union club official on the plethora
> of representative and trial matches.

●

I earn every penny.

> **Lawrie McMenemy**, justifying his £166,078.00
> salary as Sunderland's managing director.

●

I only earn half as much as Bobby Robson and
a third as much as Sunderland's Lawrie McMenemy.

> **Brian Clough**, explaining his decision to carry on
> after earlier saying he would retire from football
> management at 50.

●

The League pay is pretty good. Money is a great
incentive in sport. In fact to be truthful it's the only
reason I'm doing it. I'd rather be catching pigs any
day.

> **Noel 'Crusher' Cleal**, Australian second row
> forward and boar hunter.

●

His country of origin does not make him a world
beater alone. He is Australian, but so is Rolf Harris.

> *Whitehaven News* introducing the local rugby
> league club's new import.

Oh, Ay, we've got a plan. We've had one all along. It's just that we haven't been able to use t'booger.

Maurice Bamford, then GB rugby league coach, after the two thrashings by Australia.

●

When I was younger, yeah, sure, I used to make love, go training, make love, fight and then make love again. But now I'm champion of the world I can't do that. I've got to set an example to young kids. But I'm not reformed.

Lloyd Honeyghan, world welterweight champion.

●

I like being famous and being on television and being successful. It's compensation for all the awful wet Mondays on no-hopers at Leicester or Wolverhampton.

Steve Smith Eccles, National Hunt jockey and author.

●

Listen I'm not going to carry the can for this club's failure to win the title.

Ron Atkinson, Manchester United manager, in September. He was no more successful a prophet than a manager. He was sacked a month later.

●

Some of the fans see me as the new messiah, but I like to say to my players: 'one day you're the greatest, the next you're a plonker.'

Terry Yorath, Swansea City manager.

●

A young bloke swore at a policeman. The kid ran away, and was caught and locked up for the night. I told the boy I was fining him, not for swearing, but for allowing a copper to catch him. I told him as a young, fit player he should be ashamed of himself. The kid just creased up laughing. That's management.

Alan Ball, Portsmouth manager.

●

Oh well, back to work tomorrow morning – nine

Now it's his turn to enjoy himself. He's having his first bitch tomorrow.

Cliff Kevern, owner of world-beating greyhound, Ballyregan Bob.

o'clock sharp. But I might go in wearing my silver medal.

Richard Leman, England hockey player, after the World Cup.

●

When I need to talk business with people, they only want to talk hockey. Also more girls want to talk to me. My girlfriend finds that a pain.

Sean Kerly, England's star forward, on the hockey World Cup's impact.

●

We need to lose our middle-class image. I'd like to see kids playing this game in the streets of Liverpool.

Ian Taylor, England goalkeeper, on hockey's

prospects of capitalising on its popularity after the World Cup.

●

I don't want to push my luck. Everybody has only got one neck.

Alan Melville, England rugby union captain, announcing his retirement.

●

Away games are more like school outings. We have problems with acne rather than injuries.

Brian Clough on the youth of his Forest side leading the First Division in the autumn.

●

My mum wants the season to end tomorrow.

Dave Bassett as Wimbledon briefly topped the First Division.

●

You must remember, man, one beautiful day doesn't make a summer.

Viv Richards after the West Indies' defeat by Pakistan.

●

We offer no excuses, though the shower of cans, eggs, nuts and bolts through the match did not help my team.

Leo Beenhakker, Real Madrid coach, after defeat by Osasuna.

●

I'm just waiting for Pavarotti to blast out of the speakers.

Elise Burgin, US Wightman Cup captain, arriving at the Albert Hall.

●

Last night I had a nightmare about a round building, filled with people making a lot of noise, and I woke in a cold sweat.

Sara Gomer, British tennis player after losing to Kathy Rinaldi.

It's mental for a Test team to carry a soft toy about. I can see Vince Karalins walking out to play Australia carrying a silly toy lion – he'd tell them what to do with it.

Ian Clift, Swinton rugby league chairman, on Great Britain's lion mascot.

●

The relationship between the Welsh and English is based on trust and understanding. They don't trust us and we don't understand them.

Dudley Wood, RFU secretary.

●

When I'm in charge of Welsh clubs, I have to whip them like animals.

Roger Quittenton, English rugby union referee, after heated match between London Welsh and Newport.

●

Let he who is without sin cast the first stone. I haven't heard a bloody ripple yet.

Ray Prosser, Pontypool coach, on the prosecution of Pontypool half-back David Bishop for assault. Bishop knocked Chris Jarman out with a punch.

●

Overall I hope it's Newport.

Bishop, while awaiting to hear whether his appeal against a one month gaol sentence had been successful. The alternative to prison was Pontypool's visit to Newport.

●

I bear no grudge, but I don't think I'll share a pint with him.

Chris Jarman, Bishop's victim, on hearing of Bishop's gaol sentence.

●

Violence on the rugby field is a bore.

Denis Thatcher, former rugby union referee.

147

I could go out and buy Henry Cooper if I wanted
a player like that.

David Pleat, Spurs manager, on John Fashanu
after a brawling match at White Hart Lane.

●

It was a case of handbags at three paces and he
was unlucky.

John Hollins, Chelsea manager, after Doug
Rougvie was sent off for tangling with Fashanu.

●

My lads went bonkers over this. They don't want
queers and lesbians in the changing rooms.

Jim Tripp, Ealing Town FC chairman, on a
council edict requiring positive discrimination from
grant recipients.

●

We don't want a reputation as an attractive team
that doesn't win matches.

Viv Anderson, Arsenal full-back.

●

It will be all downhill for him from now on. Leaving
Manchester United is like leaving the Hilton and
booking in at some run-down little hotel round the
corner.

Tommy Docherty on Ron Atkinson's dismissal.

●

When I got the job I said I was going to approach
it in a laid-back manner. Laid back? I found myself
screaming during games, shaking with nervousness on
the touchline. I've become like all the other half-witted
managers.

Graeme Souness, Rangers manager.

●

I get a lot of stick from rival fans, who call me a
wife batterer, but I can handle that. It's when you get
fellow-pros doing the same thing that it's upsetting.

Mark Dennis, Southampton full-back, on his
tenth sending off. His matrimonial disputes had
been receiving press attention.

In the past there were wars. For a thousand years
we needed tough young fellows like this, prepared to
shed blood at the drop of a hat.

> **Keith Evans**, defence counsel in the Chelsea
> hooligans trial.

●

Yesterday I was selling toothpaste. Now I must learn
about a fresh product.

> **Trevor Phillips**, new commercial director of the
> Football League.

Family football is a fallacy. On a Saturday afternoon
in February women want to curl up in front of a film
in their centrally heated house.

> **Ted Croker**, FA Secretary.

●

I can't believe he said that.

> **Linda Whitehead**, WFA Secretary, replying to
> her male opposite number.

●

I don't like the Luton idea. I may be naive, but
I like to hear cheers and counter-cheers.

> **Maxwell Holmes**, Leeds United director, on
> Luton's ban on away fans.

●

I can cope with being thrown out of the Labour Party,
I can cope with losing my job with Knowsley Council,
but I can't cope with Liverpool beating Everton 4–1
and Ian Rush scoring a hat-trick.

> **Derek Hatton.**

●

Artificial pitches might be good for individual clubs,
but they are no damned good for the game. Let those
clubs that want them break away from the League.
They can ban visiting supporters if they so wish, they
can call themselves the 'David Evans League' if they
like, but for God's sake leave the rest of us alone.

> **Howard Kendall**, Everton manager, on the plastic

clubs threat of legal action to protect their status.
Evans was Luton chairman.

●

Wolves may be Fourth Division, but what a name!
Mick Weatherman, Chorley secretary, on the
FA Cup draw which paired his non-League side
with Wolves. Chorley eventually won 3–0.

●

The most enjoyable part of the last 12 months has
been the three weeks I spent digging the garden when
I was between jobs.
Graham Turner, Wolves and ex-Aston Villa
manager, after FA Cup defeat by Chorley.

●

Life's full of meetings now. I never used to have
anything to have a meeting about.
Joe Johnson, World Snooker champion, explaining why he'd managed only 18 hours' practice in
the 12 weeks after winning the championship.

●

I'm gutted – I keep losing to wallies.
Eric Bristow, after defeat in the World Matchplay
Darts Championships.

●

There's only one wally in this tournament – and
he's back at home.
Jocky Wilson replying to Bristow.

●

Frankly, I'd rather have a drink with Idi Amin.
Alex Higgins on Steve Davis.

●

We accepted very generous donations while we were
there.
Colin Meads, coach to the unofficial New Zealand
Cavaliers rugby side in South Africa.

●

It was always thought that members would fight
with gloves on.
Bob Weighill, Secretary of the International

Rugby Board, on South Africa's ignoring the
ban on the Cavaliers tour.

●

The people are like hungry wolves. If you throw
them some meat, they want more.
Dr Danie Craven, South Africa Rugby Board
chairman, on the growing pressure for more 'rebel'
tours after the visit by the Cavaliers.

●

We see rugby tours as important to our international
position.
Stoffel van der Merwe, Deputy head of the
SA National Party information division.

●

I remember praying 'Lord thy will be done.' Afterwards
I was thrilled by the answer to the prayer and by how
the Lord had used me as a witness in this way.
Meredith Marshall on winning the Scottish
Ladies Open Golf Championship.

●

It was up to them to attack. After all, they were
at home.
Sandro Altobelli, Internazionale Milan forward,
after 0–0 draw with AC Milan. The teams share
the San Siro stadium.

●

I am a passionate man. I go home and cry. I get
pains in my chest because my team are not playing
well enough.
Peter Fox, Leeds rugby league coach.

●

Many clubs have expressed concern about the trans-
mission of Aids, but our doctor has assured them that
the game of rugby is a perfectly safe activity from this
threat.
Dudley Wood, RFU Secretary.

I have his strategy all figured out now – he hits
the ball, you chase it.

Mike Way, Canadian squash player, after losing
9–0, 9–1, 9–0 to Jahangir Khan.

•

We must all learn to play in the human league before
we play in the god league. So don't anyone talk about
beating him.

Jan-Ulf Soderberg, after winning only two points
from Jahangir.

•

I might catch a little if there isn't a ball game to watch.

Ronald Reagan, U.S. President, asked whether
he proposed to watch the televised Congressional
Irangate hearings.

•

Passengers are reminded that they should be as quiet
as possible during this trip because Mike Gatting is
trying to catch up on his sleep.

Air Hostess on the Melbourne to Adelaide flight.
Gatting, the new England captain, had arrived late
for play in the Melbourne Test after oversleeping.

•

Hobbs, Hammond and Broad: it doesn't quite ring
true, does it?

Chris Broad on becoming the third Englishman
to score centuries in three successive Tests in a
series in Australia.

•

We're not going to just hang the man. We're going
to give him a fair trial . . . then we'll hang him.

Jose Torres, New York Boxing Commissioner,
on Tim Witherspoon's positive response to a drug
test. It was later found to be negative.

1987

I blame Shilton for that Maradona goal. I would
have taken him *and* the ball.

> **Dick Pym**, 94-year-old former Bolton goalkeeper
> and sole survivor of the first Wembley Cup final
> in 1923.

●

That's life, that's darts, that's pressure. I can't
complain. He done me. The only person that won
out there was darts.

> **Eric Bristow**, the 'Crafty Cockney', after world
> final defeat by John Lowe.

●

I wouldn't say God couldn't have got it out, but
he'd have had to throw it.

> **Arnold Palmer** on the bunker lie at the hole
> where he took 10 at the Open.

●

Everybody thinks we should have moustaches and
hairy arses, but in fact you could put us all on the
front of *Vogue*.

> **Helen Kirk** of the Deers women's rugby union
> team.

●

The manners of rugby [union] players are impeccable
compared with those of, say, motorists on the M25.

> **Roger Quittenton**, English referee.

●

I am not proud of what I did, especially as I am
a policeman.

> **Wade Dooley**, England rugby union forward,
> after breaking cheekbone of Wales' Phil Davies.

I think we could find a place for Dooley as a bouncer
at our social club.
   Alex Murphy, St Helens rugby league coach.
   ●
I can go faster.
   Ben Johnson, Canadian sprinter, after breaking
   the world record for 100m by a tenth of a second.
   ●
I feel a strange air at these [world athletics] champi-
onships. A lot of people have just come out of nowhere
and are running unbelievably. The drugs problem is
worse than ever.
   Carl Lewis.
   ●
Well done Dennis Connor – you old bastard!
   Australian banner as Stars & Stripes won
   sailing's America's Cup.
   ●
Swearing at the polo club? It's a load of bollocks.
   Major Ronald Ferguson, denying that Prince
   Charles had used bad language in a chukkah.
   ●
He did not give the referee two fingers. He put
one finger up twice.
   Mark Newton, Bracknell basketball club spokes-
   man, defending a player sent off.
   ●
Gatting used some filthy language to the umpire.
Let me tell you some less filthy words are 'bastard'
and 'son of a bitch'. No one has a right to abuse umpires.
   General Safdar Butt, president of Pakistan crick-
   et board, on the Gatting-Rana confrontation.
   ●
Pakistan have been cheating us for 37 years and it
is getting worse. It was bad enough when I toured in
'51. The TCCB should bring the boys home.
   Tom Graveney, ex-England batsman.

I can tell thee, Reagan meeting Gorbachev is nowt compared wi' this.

Dickie Bird, umpire, on the Gatting-Rana altercation.

●

The Football League is run by small men with even smaller minds. They have shown the impartiality, wisdom and far-sightedness of a committee of Pakistani umpires.

Robert Maxwell, Derby County chairman.

●

This is a bad way to get famous.

Bobby Frankham, boxer banned *sine die* for hitting referee at Wembley.

●

I wish I had put ballet shoes on him and not boxing gloves.

Hazel Frankham, Bobby's mum.

●

I work in the City where a lot of people react to the pressure by taking cocaine. I prefer rugby league.

Bob Evans, Fulham RL fan on being named national Supporter of the Year.

●

When they see Mirandinha, every club will want a Brazilian.

Don Packham, football agent, on Newcastle's South American signing, who was to last barely two seasons.

●

Arsenal keep hitting that 6ft 4in Irishman [Niall Quinn] with high balls and it's quality football. We hit a 6ft 3in black fella [John Fashanu] on the head and it's violence.

Dave Bassett, Wimbledon manager.

●

I can still go out as long as it's after midnight, I'm

wearing dark glasses and it's a dimly lit restaurant.
Terry Venables, prior to his dismissal as Barcelona manager.

●

It was an orgasm of personal bests – and I won.
Ed Moses, USA's world 400m hurdles champion.

●

It was rather like watching Arsenal v Spurs on *Match of the Day*. You don't get any of the dross, only the highlights.
David Spens, defending counsel in the Cynthia Payne sex-parties trial.

●

The best feeling in the world – even better than sex.
Derek Redmond, UK athlete, on the final dash for the line over 400m.

●

With our luck, one of our players must be bonking a witch.
Ken Brown, Norwich City manager, on his team's wretched form.

●

Muirfield without a wind is like a lady undressed. No challenge.
Tom Watson, American golfer, at the Open Championship.

●

I gave up smoking at 13 when I discovered more exciting ways of losing my breath.
David Bulstrode, QPR chairman, at *Rothmans Football Yearbook* launch.

●

Gary Wager's safer than a condom.
Merthyr Tydfil football fans' banner at European Cup-Winners' Cup game at Bergamo, Italy.

●

Stayed in your wine bar, you should've stayed in your wine bar . . .
Spurs' Fans' song to Watford's stand-in goal-

keeper, barman Gary Plumley, at FA Cup semi-final won 4–1 by Tottenham.

•

Now we shall be shopping at Harrod's as well as Woolworth's.

John Sillett, Coventry City manager, after beating Spurs to win the Cup.

•

The offer he made for David Speedie suggests he is trying to shoplift from Harrod's.

Ken Bates, Chelsea chairman. Speedie later joined Coventry for £750,000.

•

You think my run-up was long. You should hear my speeches.

Wes Hall, West Indies bowler-turned-politician.

•

Leningrad must be spinning in his grave.

Don King, US boxing promoter, on a rival's plans to promote in the Soviet Union.

•

We never defect to Tunisia, and never at lunchtime.

Soviet official after computer error had turned a Russian swimmer into a Tunisian.

•

He runs twice a day – from the freezer to the bathroom.

Mike Ditka, Chicago Bears American football coach, warning William 'The Refrigerator' Perry to lose weight.

•

Then my eyesight started to go, and I took up refereeing.

Neil Midgley, FA Cup final referee.

•

I can see the sun OK – and it's 93 million miles away.

Bruce Froemming, US baseball umpire, to a player who questioned his eyesight.

It was like robbing a bank and dropping the money
. . . he was already posing for the photographers when
he went over.

> **Alex Murphy**, St Helens rugby league coach,
> on Mark Elia's bungled try attempt in Wembley
> defeat by Halifax.

●

Contrary to public opinion, I don't tell my players
to kick the opposition in the nuts.

> **Dave Bassett**, manager of controversial Wim-
> bledon FC.

●

We held them for 89 minutes, then they kippered us.

> **Dogan Arif**, manager of non-League Fisher
> Athletic FC, after losing to Telford.

●

If I played tennis like the umpires judge I would
be ranked 5,000th in the world.

> **John McEnroe**.

●

I don't want a brat. If John isn't strict with him,
then I will be.

> **Tatum O'Neal**, McEnroe's wife, on baby Kevin
> John.

●

McEnroe's problem is not injuries, but a failure to
live with the reality that he is no longer the best.

> **Mats Wilander**, Swedish tennis player, on
> McEnroe's withdrawal from Wimbledon.

●

Other girls my age think about boys, boys, boys.
I think tennis, tennis, tennis.

> **Steffi Graf**, West German teenage prodigy.

●

My guitar and tennis racquet are no longer the
most important things in my life.

> **Pat Cash**, new Wimbledon champion, on father-
> hood.

I'm not immortal. I didn't lose a war, nobody died.
I only lost a tennis match.
>   **Boris Becker** after second-round defeat by 500–1
>   outsider Peter Doohan at Wimbledon.

●

Twenty per cent off all Becker goods.
>   **Shop sign** at Wimbledon, after the West German's
>   defeat.

●

If I went out to practise with Becker when the women's
final was on, people would watch the knock-up.
>   **Pat Cash**, trashing women's tennis.

●

Keep working on your serve and volley and you
could make a living on the women's circuit.
>   **Martina Navratilova** to Cash.

●

Good women riders don't lose races because they
are weaker, they lose because they are on the worst
horses.
>   **Lorna Vincent**, National Hunt jockey.

●

Winning was as easy as sitting in a movie theatre.
>   **Said Aouita**, Moroccan long-distance runner.

●

At the end of the day, it's not the end of the world.
>   **Jim McLean**, Dundee United manager, after
>   losing the first leg of the UEFA Cup final to
>   Gothenberg.

●

We know that Ian Rush lets his goals do the talking,
but so far he hasn't spoken very much.
>   **Gianni Agnelli**, Juventus president, on the Welsh
>   striker's poor run in Italy.

●

I *hate* swimming.
>   **Sarah Hardcastle**, British swimmer, announcing
>   her retirement.

159

I'm a bit different from the Australian players
of the past. Can you imagine any of them
wearing a diamond earring?

Pat Cash after victory in the Wimbledon
men's final.

It would be like giving more drink to an alcoholic.

> **Barry Batey**, Sunderland director, opposing a plan
> to give big-spending manager Lawrie McMenemy
> more cash for players.

●

Fifty caps or £100,000 – I know which I would rather
have.

> **Jonathan Davies**, a year before leaving Welsh
> rugby union for Widnes rugby league.

●

The only place Seve [Ballesteros] turns up for nothing
is at his Mum's for breakfast.

> **Howard Clark**, Yorkshire golfer, on his Ryder
> Cup team-mate.

●

It may not look nice, but I've never seen anyone
score from Row Z of the stand.

> **Mick McCarthy** on a Manchester City team-
> mate's failure to hoof a ball clear, which led to
> the winning goal against them.

●

Five out of 10 for football, 11 out of 10 for character.

> **Arthur Cox**, Derby County manager, on his
> team's fightback to win after trailing 2–0 to
> Barnsley.

●

Hey, this is not a game for well-adjusted individuals.

> **Bill Parcells**, coach to New York Giants American
> football team, after being attacked by a player.

●

Nobody in American football is going to suffer from
the odd forearm smash or an elbow in the face.

> **Len Casey**, Hull rugby league coach.

●

The weather was far from pleasant, so were the
opposition, so were the media.

> **England Selectors'** confidential report to Test
> & County Cricket Board after Pakistan's tour.

A horse used to wander in from a nearby field and eat my mum's washing. One day instead of leading it away, I jumped on him and rode him back to the field. From then on I was hooked.

Ray Cochrane on how he became a jockey.

●

My golf swing is a lot like ironing a shirt. You get one side smoothed out, turn it over and there is a big wrinkle on the other side. Then you iron that out, turn it over and there is another big wrinkle.

Tom Watson on going 47 tournaments without a win.

●

If he [Ian Woosnam] ever grows up, he'll be one hell of a player.

Seve Ballesteros, Spanish golfer.

●

I've had to swap my Merc for a BMW, I'm down to my last 37 suits and I'm drinking non-vintage champagne.

Ron Atkinson on life after his dismissal as Manchester United manager.

●

I've had these barren spells before. What's the Spanish for it? *El blanko runno* I suppose.

Gary Lineker, England striker, struggling for goals at Barcelona.

●

I go to a party on Friday night, sometimes until 4am, then score 50 and take five wickets.

Omar Henry, the first Coloured cricketer chosen to play for South Africa.

●

I took a basketball to bed until I was 14. You don't see that kind of dedication any more.

Pete Maravich, American ex-player, on being inducted into the Hall of Fame.

Sometimes I wake up on Sunday mornings and even my eyelids ache.

John Perkins, Pontypool rugby union captain, announcing his retirement at 32.

●

What do I think of the reverse sweep? It's like Manchester United getting a penalty and Bryan Robson taking it with his head.

David Lloyd, former Lancashire and England cricketer.

●

Too much cricket will kill cricketers before they are ready to be killed.

Mike Gatting, England captain.

●

No Iron Bottom?

Passer-by in Rawalpindi, addressing England cricket tourists on the absence of Botham.

●

It was the best and worst day of my life.

Brian Miller, Burnley FC manager, on his club's last-gasp escape from relegation into non-League football.

●

The Brazilians love that football more than a man loves a sweet new bride.

Martti Kuusela, Finland manager.

●

Not bad for the worst team ever to leave England.

Mike Gatting on his Test team's grand slam in Australia.

●

You could fulfil your dream, then be branded a scab for the rest of your life.

Ron Roberts, London Ravens quarterback, rejecting an offer to break the American football strike.

●

They talk about some of the wild men in Spain, but I

don't think any of their hatchet men would be able to
live with some of ours.

> **Jim McLean**, Dundee United manager, on the
> Scottish Premier Division.

●

Two things mean nothing in baseball – last year
and yesterday.

> **Whitey Herzog**, St Louis Cardinals manager.

●

What did I learn playing for Richmond? How to
drink beer.

> **Seiji Hirao**, Japanese rugby union player.

●

What we see today is the product of too many players
drinking and staying out late too much.

> **Ron Saunders**, West Bromwich Albion manager.

●

We had a skinful last night. Work hard, play hard.

> **Steve Coppell**, Crystal Palace manager, after
> his team had beaten West Brom.

●

He's taken loads of chunks out of me over the years.
I give him a carrot every night – and he still hates
me.

> **Nicky Henderson**, trainer of triple champion
> hurdler See You Then.

●

This makes up for all the crap I've taken over the
years. I was close to perfect.

> **Phil Simms**, New York Giants quarterback, voted
> Super Bowl's Most Valuable Player.

●

We beat the Pope!

> **Michael Fay**, New Zealand's America's Cup syn-
> dicate chief, on the turn-out for their ticker-tape
> welcome in Auckland.

●

I live in hope that one day I'll go along to a youth
match, as in 1963, watch an unknown kid for five

164

minutes and find myself asking: 'My God – who *is* that?'

> **Pat Crerand**, former Manchester United and Scotland player, on football's search for another George Best.

●

In my day there were plenty of footballers around who would kick your bollocks off. The difference was that at the end they would shake your hand and help you look for them.

> **Nat Lofthouse**, former Bolton and England centre-forward, on football in the post-War years.

●

Jesus Christ, 60 per cent of all the Aussies I know think Joe Bugner is something you find up the Queensland premier's nose.

> Letter to *New Australasian Express*.

●

His heart is as big as a pea.

> **Henry Cooper**, ex-boxer, on Bugner.

●

Frank [Bruno] is a nice enough fella. But he's muscle-bound, can't fight and has a dodgy chin.

> **Terry Downes**, ex-British fighter.

●

I've been booed since 1971, so I've got used to the sound.

> **Joe Bugner** before fighting Bruno at Tottenham.

●

I'm retiring now – let them find someone else to boo.

> **Joe Bugner** after losing.

●

I like to think we're Saint and Greavsie with completed sentences.

> **Desmond Lynam** on his TV double act with Gerry Williams at Wimbledon tennis championships.

Herol [Graham] has just boxed like a horse that's been nobbled.

Barney Eastwood, boxing manager, after Graham's European title defeat by Sambu Kalamby of Italy.

●

Graham has turned defensive boxing into a poetic art. Trouble is, no one was ever knocked out by a poem.

Eddie Shaw, boxing trainer.

●

One problem was that gentlemen with white and brown faces confronted each other determined to have a punch-up. I've never seen it before on a Test cricket ground, and I hope I never see it again.

Raman Subba Row, Test & County Cricket Board chairman, after crowd trouble at England v Pakistan game at Edgbaston.

●

It hasn't really sunk in that I'm champion again. It probably will when I sober up. Now I intend to get paralytic – that's how much winning means to me.

Steve Davis, after winning World Snooker Championship.

●

The bell went ding and I went dong.

Lloyd Honeyghan, British boxer, on knocking down Johnny Bumphus with first punch of second round in his world-title defence.

●

They earn all that money yet not one of them would buy you a cup of coffee.

Bernie Ecclestone, head of Brabham's F-1 motor-racing team, on drivers' reluctance to pay a licence levy.

●

Bonecrusher just came to stink the joint out.

Kevin Rooney, Mike Tyson's trainer, after James

It's new, it's dangerous . . . it's Tysonitis.
Don King, US boxing promoter, on his
awesome heavyweight.

'Bonecrusher' Smith's defeat in an uneventful world-title bout.

●

Sure I fought to survive. Wouldn't you?
   'Bonecrusher' Smith, American heavyweight, to the media.

●

I was in the corner when [Nigel] Mansell came in. I could see he was not coming to apologise. His face was not right for that. You don't come to say you're sorry when you grab somebody by the throat.
   Ayrton Senna, Brazilian driver, after his collision with Mansell in Belgian Grand Prix.

●

I look at some of the players around today and I bloody well weep. That Mark Hateley – they're talking about spending millions on him, but the poor bloke can't play the game. Couldn't trap a dead rat, yet he's made a fortune.
   Stan Bowles, ex-England footballer.

●

If there was a revolution in this country now, I'd be in the first 10,000 to the guillotine. But not the first 1,000.
   J.J. Warr on being elected President of the MCC.

●

I've got nothing to say. No one at our club is allowed to say anything.
   Stuart Pearce of Nottingham Forest on winning his first England cap.

●

Mansell handles corners better than Maradona.
   Banner at British motor-racing grand prix.

●

Sugar Ray Leonard's retirements last about as long as Liz Taylor's marriages.
   Bob Arum, US boxing promoter.

●

I only wish some of the players' trousers fitted better.
   Duke of Edinburgh on modern cricket.

1988

In sport it would be nice if we could recover our reputation and in soccer once again become the gentleman of Europe.

Mrs Thatcher's new year message.

●

I can imagine the likes of Real Madrid and Juventus coming down to Plough Lane to play us. I don't think they would like it too much.

Vinnie Jones, Wimbledon player, looking forward to his side's prospects of qualifying for Europe in January.

●

Ardiles was the difference – it was like trying to tackle dust.

Joe Royle, Oldham manager, after his side's 4–2 third round FA Cup defeat by Spurs.

●

Sometimes you have to stamp your authority on a game, but I went a bit too far.

Andy Sennett, Cheshire referee, banned for swearing at a schoolboy player.

●

There won't be any topless teams.

Paul Raymond, Soho nightclub owner, trying to buy Watford FC.

●

I never intended selling my soul to the devil.

Elton John deciding not to sell Watford.

The only people going to get caught are the stupid ones, or the ones who don't matter.

Daley Thompson on the Amateur Athletic Association's enquiry into drug-taking.

●

I don't believe there was only one athlete on drugs at the World Championships in Rome.

Carl Lewis, the American sprinter, insisting that drug taking was prevalent in Athletics.

●

I saw Carl straight after his 100 metres defeat against Ben Johnson in the World Championships and he was at one of the lowest points of his career. At times like that, if you are not careful, you can let your imagination run away with you.

Brendan Foster dismissing Lewis's allegations.

●

It is the fetishism of the second best which prevails in France. If you go down the Loire Valley you see all those grand castles. They look impressive from the outside with their spectacular walls and fortifications. But they are empty inside. There is nothing behind those impressive facades. This was the story of French rugby: plenty of flourishes, but we kept losing. It was a sham.

Jacques Fouroux, the French coach, before France v England in Paris.

●

Have you seen the pitch? It is like the moon's surface.

Jackie Hendriks, West Indies manager, after his side scored 147–5 v India at Madras.

●

The wicket was helpful, but I had to bowl and plan.

Narendra Hirwani, Indian leg-spinner, after taking a record Test debut 16–136 in Madras.

●

Both team manager Mickey Stewart and Mike Gatting have given us assurances this week that dissent will not occur again. Players cannot behave as they did in

Pakistan even if the provocation was immense.

Raman Subba Row, TCCB chairman, before
the England tour of New Zealand and Australia.

●

The Pakistan tour is finished, and we want it dead
and buried.

Peter Lush, England tour manager, arriving in
New Zealand.

●

Pakistan have been cheating us for 37 years. And
by us, I mean other countries as well as England.

Mike Gatting in Australia 2 weeks later.

●

Now we know how Gatting felt.

Anonymous England rugby player after England
lost 10–9 to France thanks to a disallowed try.

●

A vulgar display of power and wealth in places where
men continue to die of hunger and thirst.

L'Osservatore Romano, the Vatican official newspaper, on the Paris-Dakar Rally.

●

You can't make deals with such people.

Martina Navratilova complaining about the
organisers of the Australian Open Championships
allowing Aboriginal Protesters to demonstrate
inside the stadium.

●

I'd say that perhaps other people hadn't seen the
anguish out there. I'd never seen such an unhappy
bunch of blokes in my life. In view of the exceptional
circumstances of the tour, I thought the payment was
warranted.

Raman Subba Row, chairman of the TCCB,
defending his payment of a £1,000 'bad behaviour' bonus to the 1987 England touring team
in Pakistan. The TCCB executive committee had
subsequently condemned it.

By gum, I thought everybody would have long forgotten the likes of me.

Tom Finney, honoured by football writers.

●

I have just seen hope going over the horizon with its backside on fire.

Miss Paddy O'Connor, racehorse trainer, who missed the chance of her first winner in four years when jockey eased up.

●

I'm a graduate of three universities – women, booze, the track.

Charles Bukowski, American writer, on his love of racing captured in a film, *Barfly*.

●

Playing American football is like being in a car accident every week.

Howie Long, 19st 4lb linebacker with the LA Raiders.

●

Last week I was a black quarterback who wanted to be good. Today I'm a good quarterback who happens to be black.

Doug Williams, Redskin, Super Bowl's first black quarterback and voted Most Valuable Player.

●

In the Ruhr region [of West Germany] people are out of work. In Afghanistan there is a terrible refugee problem. But there are still people who talk about Boris Becker's crisis.

Becker.

●

No thanks, give it to sport.

News editor of ABC radio network when told by correspondent the United States had been awarded the 1994 World Cup.

A country where millions of people are starving and which has the Third World's largest foreign debt cannot consider the sponsorship of a World Cup with government money.

> **Pele** on why Brazil should not stage the finals.

●

It is an honour to be given the No.10 shirt. It always weighs a bit more than the rest.

> **Luciano**, Brazil under-15 player burdened by the Pele legend.

●

My wife says it would be better if there was another woman, at least then she would know what she was up against. But she says, 'How can I compete with a football?'

> **Don Mackay**, Blackburn Rovers manager.

●

Today is without doubt the biggest of my life. My wife thinks it was when we got married.

> **John Emery**, chairman of Gordon League rugby union club, after narrow cup defeat by Waterloo.

●

The New Zealand Government cannot stop her coming, but she is not going to be welcome. Her home is South Africa, white South Africans regard her as one of their own.

> **Peter Tapsell**, New Zealand Minister for Sport, on Zola Budd's selection for the British team in the World Cross Country Championships in Auckland.

●

She has abused her flag of convenience by not living here. She has taken us all for a ride.

> **Ron Pickering**, Athletics Coach and TV commentator.

●

I hope everybody now will accept that I have completely cut my ties with South Africa. I am proud to be a Briton and will do my best for Britain.

> **Zola Budd** insisting again that she had cut her

links with South Africa in February.

●

I've got 6 CSEs, and this has to be a better opportunity than hoping for a job with the water authority.

Martin Charters, 16, waiting to hear if he had been accepted for the first cricket YTS programme.

●

I know I'm better than most people I play in Ramsgate, but I didn't realise I was world class.

Richard Bean, video shop owner, on winning the World Poker Championship in Las Vegas.

●

Don King doesn't care about black or white. He just cares about green.

Larry Holmes.

●

Hey, I earned $3 million tonight. That's what I fight for. I'm a professional. If they'd said 'do it for free' I wouldn't have showed up.

Larry Holmes, after his heavy beating by Mike Tyson.

●

I'd kick my own brother if necessary. That's what being a professional is all about.

Steve McMahon, Liverpool and England midfield player.

●

They were like West Ham used to be – all fancy flicks and sweet sherry.

Phil Sproson, Port Vale defender, after their FA Cup fourth round victory over Spurs.

●

I just wish that I could go to the supermarket and buy 11 pairs of fresh legs for the replay.

Frank Connor, the Raith Rovers manager, on their Scottish Cup battles against Rangers.

I don't want to be egotistical, but I don't think there's
a man on the planet who can beat me.
Mike Tyson.

●

I know people are going to laugh at me and think
I'm boasting, but every time I see Mike Tyson I fancy
him more and more. I'm not a 38-year-old grandfather
who's been out of the ring for two years.
Frank Bruno.

●

I don't think they've been at our club since decimali-
sation. But then, I don't think I'd know them even if
they did turn up.
Gwent rugby club official on the Wales selectors'
apparent bias towards the Western clubs.

●

We don't have to believe the Welsh myth that just
because players pull on a red shirt they become
different animals imbued with magical powers.
Geoff Cooke, England manager before the rugby
international at Twickenham. Wales won.

●

I hope my successor gets more help from the secretary
than I did.
Mike England, after being sacked as manager
by Wales.

●

I can't promise to give the team talk in Welsh,
but from now on I shall be taking my holidays in
Porthcawl and I've a complete set of Harry Secombe
albums.
Brian Clough, after being offered the Wales job.

●

I am boiling about what happened today and I'm
going home to think about my next move. I'm going
to sleep on it. And if I wake up in the morning still
thinking of quitting I'll sleep on it again. And if the

feeling remains – then I'll be off. No mucking about.

Brian Clough after the Forest directors refused him permission to accept the Welsh job part-time.

●

I'm going nowhere. Resignations are for prime ministers and cabinets, and those caught with their trousers down, not for me.

Clough after sleeping on it two days later. ·

●

I'm not one of nature's headbangers. I find I don't need all that macho mayhem before a game.

Dean Richards, England No.8 and policeman, on his pre-match preparations.

●

Anyone connected with the game at whatever level can think back to times in their playing career when the property belonging to others was abused, broken or stolen.

David Hands, *Times* rugby correspondent, on the suspension of Richards and Scottish flanker John Jeffrey after £1,000 damage was done to the Calcutta Cup at the post match revelries.

●

It will now have to be called the Calcutta Shield.

Bob Munro, Scotland's World Cup rugby manager, on the damage caused to the famous Cup.

●

They came to do a job, but at what cost to rugby I just don't know. They played to slow the game down by whatever means possible. You can call it gamesmanship – I think the fashionable word is streetwise.

Derrick Grant, Scotland coach, after England's 9–6 victory at Murrayfield.

●

I'm still too upset to think much about what I'm going to do, but I may take up Karate.

Trevor Harris, Exeter RFC tighthead prop, on

being suspended for 13 months after being sent
off a fifth time.

●

It is a great shame, because they are such a fine
team – but Heysel was more than a great shame.
Hans Bangerter, UEFA secretary, on Liverpool's
European isolation.

●

If we were doing all this in the Falklands they
would love it. It's part of our heritage. The British
have always been fighting wars.
Fan on hooliganism charges, talking on American
TV.

●

While I was in Rio a photographer asked me to juggle
the ball on Copacabana beach. I felt so embarrassed.
We were surrounded by kids and they could juggle so
much better than me.
John Barnes.

●

I ain't doing a damn thing, and I don't start until noon.
Bum Phillips, American football coach, on how
he is spending retirement.

●

In my country you get 10 to 15 years for what
they were doing in there. It's called mugging.
Joedy Gardner, Livingstone's American coach,
after heated basketball match with Kingston.

●

While the name Manchester United has its advantages,
the association with football connects basketball with
violence and thuggery.
Richard Kay, one of consortium taking over the
Manchester basketball club when United pulled
out.

●

I'VE SEEN A GOAL SCORED AGAINST LIVER-
POOL.
I'VE SEEN LIVERPOOL BEATEN.

Liverpool supporters' badges during their record-equalling 29-game unbeaten start to the 1987–8 season.

•

You have to say they've been aided by the poorest First Division I have seen in all my years in football.
Bob Paisley, Liverpool director, on his club's run.

•

The people who come to watch us play, who love the team and regard it as part of their lives, would never appreciate Liverpool having a huge balance in the bank. They want every asset we possess to be wearing a red shirt, and that's what I want too.
Kenny Dalglish, Liverpool manager.

•

Pirmin does not ski for the money, or to be famous. His ambition is simply to be perfect on every kind of course. He loves to ski.
Marc Biver, Pirmin Zurbriggen's manager before the Winter Olympics.

•

Knowing him, nothing at all. It's just that the name Zurbriggen in future will cost rather more.
Marc Biver on the effect winning a gold medal would have on his client.

•

The guy's a bird. It's like somebody sucked all the marrow from his bones and replaced it with helium.
Matt Peri, American ski jumper, on the gold medal winner, Matti Nykaenen.

•

Eddie doesn't fly. He just drops out of the sky. It's not ski jumping.
Rob McCormack, chief of competition at Calgary ski hill, on the British ski jumper.

•

You must not laugh at Eddie, he is good for our sport. We need some clowns.
Matti Nykaenen, doyen of ski jumping.

178

Where would the Olympic Games go if Edwardses
took their place in every discipline and so discredited
the sporting achievements of all those who far outstrip
them in ability, yet not so far as to receive victory
cheers?

    Junge Welt, East Germany's Youth Newspaper.

    •

His appeal is precisely because he is such a spectacular
loser. If he had come second to last, no one would be
interested.

    Julian Brand, of the Mark McCormack agency
    IMG, explaining Edwards's great earning power.

    •

Everyone back home thinks I'm crazy. They're probably
right.

    Eddie Edwards, British ski jumper.

    •

When is all this going to end, Mrs Edwards?

    Bank manager, talking to Eddie's mother.

    •

We're here to skate in a dress and not a G-string.

    Peter Dunfield, Canadian coach, protesting over
    Witt's garb.

    •

This has been a very special match and I only hope
that what occurred has not detracted from everyone's
enjoyment.

    Chris Broad's letter of apology for knocking
    over his wicket after getting out in the Sydney
    Bicentennial Test.

    •

If players cannot behave themselves, they shouldn't
be selected to play for England.

    Raman Subba Row on Broad's behaviour.

    •

I didn't think I was the marrying type, but people
change.

    Mike Tyson, after marrying Robin Givens in
    February.

Don't worry, marriage hasn't changed this guy. He still changes the taste in your mouth quicker than anyone I know.

Rufus 'Hurricane' Hadlee, Tyson's sparring partner.

●

One-day cricket is like fast food. Nobody wants to cook.

Viv Richards, West Indies captain, after tour of India.

●

Hell's teeth, I was a bloody greyhound next to this lot.

Geoffrey Boycott on England's pedestrian batting in New Zealand.

●

Women jockeys are a pain. Jumping's a man's game. They are not built like us. Most of them are as strong as half a disprin.

Steve Smith-Eccles, National Hunt Jockey, on Gee Armytage's prospects in the Grand National 1988.

●

I cry and get so worked up. In fact, talk about Becher's Brook . . . I'm a babbling brook.

Juliet Reed, owner of Grand National winner Rhyme 'N' Reason.

●

He's had more operations than Joan Collins – and maybe more men working on him.

Jenny Pitman on Burrough Hill Lad.

●

You don't imagine I walk around looking like that all the time do you? Imagine what might happen if I wore that stuff in Portsmouth.

Bob Anderson on his 'Limestone Cowboy' gear after winning the World Darts Championship.

●

I was thinking of moving out because my manager advised me that I would save about £100,000 a year if I became a tax exile, but that was before the budget,

Every man prefers my shape to that of a rubber ball.
   Katarina Witt, East German figure-skating gold medallist.

and now there's no reason to leave.

> **Sandy Lyle**, golfer.

●

What's so great about winning in Glasgow or Cannes?
The hotels are inferior and the courses not so good.

> **Larry Nelson**, former US Open champion, as
> golfing power swung to Europeans.

●

A superstar? What's that? I still wash the dishes and
drive my own car. I am a popular player, but people
like Greg Norman and Seve Ballesteros are regarded
as superstars. They are Hollywood. The nearest I'll get
to flying a jet is a remote-controlled one.

> **Sandy Lyle** after winning the US Masters.

●

Eyes to the front, shut up, or you will be next.

> **Ian Botham** to a passenger protesting at his
> assault on another passenger, Adrian Winter, who
> had objected to Botham's language on an internal
> Australian flight. Botham was fined £320.

●

He just happened to be on the wrong plane at the
wrong time.

> **Botham** on Winter.

●

All you Aussies are a bunch of hicks who don't
know the first thing about cricket.

> **Botham**'s farewell to Australia after Queensland
> decided not to renew his contract over bad behav-
> iour.

●

I suppose it is fair to say that the ball has stopped
rolling from the general club point of view, and the
remaining games will determine its direction – the
ball that is – both the rolling one and the football.

> **Colin Murphy**, Lincoln City manager, on his
> club's promotion prospects.

●

It's difficult to know what a legend is. I find it easier

to talk about Ray Reardon in such terms. I'm a legend
in my own lunchtime, in my own break.

Steve Davis.

●

The provocation and intimidation at Anfield is incred-
ible. I can understand why clubs come away from here
choking on their own vomit, and biting their tongues,
knowing they have been done by the referee. When you
lose it sounds like sour grapes, but we got a result and
I'm saying it.

Alex Ferguson, Manchester United manager,
after his team's 3–3 draw in April.

●

You might as well talk to my daughter. You'll get
more sense out of her.

Kenny Dalglish, Liverpool manager, interrupting
Ferguson's onslaught. He was carrying his six week
old daughter.

●

He's a good penalty taker, I'll give him that. As good
as any I've seen. But I wouldn't have bought him.

Bob Paisley on Liverpool's leading scorer John
Aldridge

●

Dutch football is at its lowest ebb for years.

Arthur Cox, Derby manager, reacting to sug-
gestions that Johann Cruyff was being appointed
over his head as technical director. Within two
months PSV Eindhoven and Holland had won the
European Cup and the European Championship
respectively.

●

It wasn't political pressure or the unfair criticism that
made me leave England. I longed for Sunday lunch at
home with the family. I even longed for my favourite
food, pumpkin.

Zola Budd leaving Britain in May.

She has been such a nuisance, but I think we have now seen the back of her.

Sam Ramsamy, South African Non Racial Olympic Committee, welcoming Budd's departure.

●

I didn't even know the record existed. I just kept going.

Graeme Hick after scoring 405 not out for Worcestershire v Somerset, 19 short of A.C. MacLaren's record first-class score in England.

●

Tell me we're deliberately dirty, and you're wrong. Tell me we're tough and you're damned right.

Sam Hammam, Wimbledon's owner.

●

It was just welly, welly, welly. The ball must have been shouting for mercy.

Ron Yeats, captain of Liverpool's 1965 Cup winners, on a spying trip to watch Wimbledon.

●

We will continue to play power football. If teams don't like it we will keep stuffing it down their throats. Liverpool will be practising heading for two weeks before they play us in the FA Cup final.

Bobby Gould, Wimbledon manager.

●

They seem to think they are a law unto themselves.

Gordon Taylor, Chief Executive of the Professional Footballers' Association, on Wimbledon.

●

It's a bit like being at school with your mates.

Alan Cork on life at Plough Lane.

●

My entire flat would fit in Peter Beardsley's front room.

Jones.

●

I had to deliver the goods before I was paid big money, but kids today come into the sport and the first word they learn is 'gimme'.

Fatima Whitbread.

England have their best chance for ten years to beat the West Indies this summer.

> **Clive Lloyd** before the Test series.

●

We have not seen a match-winning performance from a bowler in Test cricket for far too long. We seem unable to bowl other sides out twice – hence we have not won many matches.

> **Peter May**, then chairman of England selectors, at the start of the 1988 season.

●

We are all on trial, including the selectors.

> **Peter May**, explaining why Gatting had only been appointed captain for the first two tests v West Indies.

●

LET'S GET THE BASTARDS.

> Wimbledon chant in the Wembley tunnel before the Cup Final.

●

People should ask where were the wonder boys of Liverpool? Why didn't they turn it on when things started to go against them? But then, they have never played well against us. They are good, but not that good.

> **Lawrie Sanchez**, scorer of Wimbledon's winning goal in the Cup Final.

●

I've never felt so bad in my life. I felt like dying because I had let so many people down – the people of Liverpool whom I love.

> **John Aldridge** after his first penalty miss of the season – in the Cup Final.

●

Going round the M25 is boring, but it gives you time to think.

> **Don Howe**, the Dons' coach, whose successful Wembley tactical plan was devised on the drive to work.

We are not panicking. There is still a lot of cricket left on this tour.

> **Viv Richards**, West Indies captain, after 3–0 defeat by England in the one day internationals.

●

ENGLAND SILENCE THEIR CRITICS
> *Times* headline after England beat West Indies 3–0 in the one-day internationals.

●

It's not my idea of glasnost.

> **Martina Navratilova** after defeat by Natalia Zvereva, of the USSR, in the French open.

●

At the milepost I thought 'I'm on the wrong one here.'

> **Ray Cochrane** after his Derby win on Kahyasi.

●

Charlie's been dropping sly innuendoes about Ben juicing up on steroids, and if it doesn't stop there'll be a massive lawsuit.

> **Mario Astophan**, Ben Johnson's doctor, on the sprinter's former coach, Charlie Francis in June.

●

TEST STARS IN SEX ORGY
> The *Sun* front page headline on 8 June which broke the story leading to the sacking of Mike Gatting after the first Test v West Indies.

●

The selectors emphasised that they did not believe the allegations (of sexual frolics) in the newspapers and accepted Gatting's account of what happened. The selectors were concerned, however, that Gatting behaved irresponsibly during a Test match by inviting female company to his room for a drink in the late evening.

> Selectors' statement removing Gatting from the England captaincy.

●

If they deny the allegations we will accept their

word as well. We do not regard this as a whitewash.

Mickey Stewart, England team manager, announcing that four other players would be interviewed at Lord's about the Nottingham hotel frolics. All denied involvement.

●

Are there any spinners playing?' asked one Leicester spectator. 'Don't mock the afflicted,' said his mate. Afflicted they certainly are. Balls keep their shine longer (with or without the application of lip gloss) so are harder to grip, and rippling muscles and chunky bats mean slow bowlers get hit much further.

Simon Hughes, Middlesex fast bowler.

●

Batsmen's technique against spin has improved out of all proportion. Trevor Bailey writes about the immaculate control of Bill O'Reilly and Clarrie Grimmett. How would they fare after being smeared over extra from leg stump or shovelled over square leg from outside off?

Simon Hughes.

●

There's too much indecision from some players – just like the manager.

Senior England player after England's 3–1 defeat by Holland in the European Championships, 1988.

●

The engine is spluttering; we just need to polish the spark plug.

Bobby Robson, England manager.

●

I will withstand the personal abuse. I will not turn it in.

Bobby Robson.

●

In this heat you simply can't afford to waste effort. Now I know how a Christmas turkey feels.

John Orwin, captaining England to rugby union tour win in Queensland.

In the five nations' they are good, but on the World platform it's like the New Zealand soccer team taking on Brazil.

Wayne Shelford, All Blacks Captain, on the Wales side which lost 52–3 to his team.

●

I was humiliated as England's captain. There was a division between the backs and forwards, who ended up blaming each other. But as a forward, I say there is no such thing as bad possession. All possession won is good ball.

John Orwin after his rugby team's unsuccessful tour of Australia.

●

At times the game resembled a duck-shooting range because of the way our blokes' heads were getting knocked off.

Wally Lewis, Australian rugby league captain, after Australia's 34–14 win in the bad-tempered second Test.

●

I fancy Starling for Christmas this year rather than turkey.

Lloyd Honeyghan, on his prospects of fighting Marlon Starling.

●

They like him here . . . because he fights like an American. That's what makes him the flash, arrogant, successful bastard he is.

Mickey Duff on Honeyghan.

●

Smile sweetly as you grind them into the ground.

Diane Bailey, British and Irish captain, to her team at the start of the Curtis Cup.

●

On days like this you get the distinct impression that someone up there likes you.

Jack Charlton, Ireland manager, after his team's

1–0 victory over England in the European Championship.

    ●

I feel embarrassed simply because I am an Englishman – it's a terrible state of mind to be in. Our clubs haven't got the earthliest chance of getting back into Europe next season.

> **Bert Millichip**, FA Chairman, on the crowd disturbances during the European Championships in Germany.

    ●

Two World Wars, One World Cup, doo-dah.

> England fans chant in Germany.

    ●

I totally disagree with the pressure coming from home that what happened in the city on Tuesday night is a reason why I should withdraw the England team from this competition. We all deplore what has happened but it's totally beyond the power of the FA to control.

> **Millichip** after events in Dusseldorf.

    ●

England play the game like old-fashioned gentlemen. Why are you so far behind the rest?

> **Igor Belanov** after USSR 3 England 1.

    ●

Going out after a week has had nothing to do with bad tactics, bad players or bad spirits – only bad finishing.

> **Bobby Robson**, England manager, after his team's failure in the European Championships.

    ●

England have some great players, but they are only great in England.

> **Leo Beenhakker**, the Real Madrid coach.

    ●

Maybe we're not as good as we thought we were.

> **Bobby Robson**, the England manager.

One of these days, we will get a rebound off a
shin-pad, and it will go in.
    Robson.
    •
When he gets mine home, he'll wonder who the
bloody hell's it is.
    Mick McCarthy, Republic of Ireland centre-half
    after swapping shirts with Ruud Gullit in the
    European Championship.
    •
Some days we could beat the London Ravens, but
on others we would lose to the Boston Bog Rolls.
    Alan Hughes, of Luton Flyers American football
    team.
    •
I would rather spend eight years in a sewer than
come back to play tennis.
    Stuart Bale, the former British No.1, after
    his defeat in the first round of the national
    championships.
    •
All of a sudden golf is very enjoyable. People are
throwing money at me. I'm even smiling at babies.
    Derrick Cooper after winning the Madrid Open.
    •
The drums, I miss the drums.
    Viv Richards on the banning of musical instru-
    ments, klaxons etc from Test grounds.
    •
Don't give up the day job, Pat.
    Des Lynam on Cash, rock singer.
    •
You were born a man, hit it like one; you can have
the operation if you want to play with the women.
    Jimmy Connors, self-critical, during defeat by
    Patrick Kuehnen on Wimbledon's graveyard No.2
    court.

It's a pain-in-the-ass court, a pain in the ass to play out there.

Jimmy Connors.

●

He is an idol, but I couldn't afford to feel sorry for him.

Patrick Kuehnen.

●

Get away from my wife! If you take her you're going to get the bills too.

Connors as his opponent, Mel Purcell, ran into the perimeter fence at Queen's Club, nearly colliding with Patti Connors.

●

Britain has got to stop looking for a player who can win Wimbledon and find 40 who may.

Tony Pickard, Stefan Edberg's coach.

●

Sod the Little Man.

Sponsor's guest at Wimbledon asked whether corporate hospitality disadvantaged the ordinary spectator.

●

Gabrielle Sabatini is very beautiful, but she walks like Robert Mitchum.

Teddy Tinling.

●

I am shy and dull. I can go about unrecognised in London. I would rather not be known by anybody. It would spoil that if I won Wimbledon.

Stefan Edberg before the men's final. He won.

●

They must learn to play off the back foot, because that is the only solution against fast bowling.

Dennis Compton on England's batting problems against West Indies, 10 July.

●

I would like to see our players getting more on to the front foot, thrusting the left pad down the pitch. It is usually fatal to try to play these West Indians off the back foot.

Sir Len Hutton, 24 July.

●

What hadn't been foreseen was that when we broke up the television cartel, any loser in that cartel would turn round and try to break up the League.

Gordon Taylor, PFA Chief Executive, on ITV's bid to finance a breakaway Super League of the top ten clubs.

●

Soccer must think it's Christmas Day.

John Bromley, head of ITV sport, after BSB and BBC had pulled out of TV 'auction'.

●

ITV appear to have scored a very expensive own goal.

Bob Hunter, of BSB.

●

The Tour de France is the only place where you can drive over the limit and get a police escort.

Raphael Gemianini, former cycling team boss.

●

There's no frogging rule for this situation.

Ken Johnson, golf official at English Amateur Championship, asked for a ruling after a frog hopped on to green.

●

The Queen is not a great cricket fan but she knew the English team were struggling a bit. She was very nice.

Mike Gatting, receiving the OBE.

●

You are going to have middle-aged women displaying thighs that should have been kept secret years ago.

Peter Coni, Henley Regatta chairman, on their clampdown on mini-skirts.

You should play every game as if it's your last, but make sure you perform well enough to make sure it's not.

> **John Emburey**, Gatting's successor as captain.

●

If you can play as if it means nothing when it means everything, you've got it.

> **Steve Davis** on secret of coping with pressure.

●

Having family caddie for you must be a bit like trying to teach the wife to drive. I know when to keep quiet.

> **Ian Wright**, hired by Ballesteros to replace brother Vicente.

●

They probably think I'm his caddie.

> **Neil Hansen**, who briefly led Ballesteros in the Mallorcan Open.

●

Trying to catch Seve is like a Chevy pick-up trying to catch a Ferrari.

> **Tom Kite**.

●

I can remember some good Saturdays against the West Indies before – the only trouble is that the Thursdays, Fridays, Mondays and Tuesdays were a bit of a disaster.

> **John Emburey** refusing to get carried away after a successful first day under his leadership in the second Test v West Indies. His caution proved justified.

●

Fixing pitches to suit the best bowlers of the home side seems to be the trend these days. I don't mind, but I hope nobody knocks us in future when we prepare wickets for our guys.

> **Viv Richards** after West Indies were greeted with a slow turner at Old Trafford. They won anyway.

193

I know nothing. I'm from Barcelona.
Seve Ballesteros, dodging a question on
his decision to live in tax-free Monte Carlo.

We didn't want to go overboard although changes had to be made.

Peter May making six changes for the Leeds Test v West Indies, including Chris Cowdrey as the third captain of the series.

●

Programme, Overseas Players and Wickets. POW.

Peter May analysing the problems of English cricket after the West Indies Test whitewash.

●

I didn't know he was the England captain, and he didn't tell me. I'm afraid I don't follow cricket, boxing's my game.

Headingley gateman who refused Chris Cowdrey admission to the ground the day before the fourth Test.

●

Sixteen needed from two overs. If we win, jubilation; if not, despair. It matters not how we played the game, but whether we won or lost.

Vic Marks on Sunday League cricket 1988.

●

He bowls too many wicket-taking balls.

England team manager **Mickey Stewart**'s analysis of Phil DeFreitas. Test statistics did not bear the analysis out.

●

It's a great honour, but it will not make any difference about my decision not to be available to tour India this winter.

Graham Gooch becoming England's fourth captain of the series v West Indies.

●

Michael [Tyson] is a manic depressive. He is. That's just a fact.

Robin Givens.

Whenever he would tell me about their arguments,
I begged him, 'Whatever happens, do not hit your wife.'
   Jose Torres, former light-heavyweight champion.

●

Frank wants to know why Tyson is messing him
around if he thinks it is such an easy fight.
   Terry Lawless.

●

He is a normal guy and car crashes happen to normal
people . . . The tree also took a 10 count.
   Steve Lott, Tyson's assistant manager.

●

At least this proves Tyson is human and can be
knocked out, even if it takes a tree to do it.
   Lawless.

●

It seems obvious they don't want to play in India.
   Margaret Alva, India's Minister for Sport, after
   Gooch withdrew from his South African commit-
   ment to lead the England touring team. The tour
   was cancelled.

●

I am still waiting to be told where I went wrong or why
I wasn't good enough after just one match. I may not
be a good enough player, or have the right leadership
qualities, but at least I deserve an explanation of where
I went wrong.
   Chris Cowdrey after being dropped as captain
   after only one test v West Indies 1988.

●

If this is the way they treat those who come and go
in the England side, no wonder we're doing so badly
and team spirit is so low. I'd heard about what went
on from other players, and now I know for myself.
   Cowdrey again.

●

It's about time some big, big men started being
honest with themselves.
   Viv Richards on England's cricket management.

196

Anyone can intellectualise about what is aesthetically acceptable football. If I had the world's best XI I would tell them to go out and play, to win 28–0 and to do it nicely.

   Howard Wilkinson on his first day as Leeds manager.

●

You can't go picking people on sentiment alone.

   Tony Ward, BAAB spokesman, insisting that Seb Coe would have to qualify for the Olympic team like everybody else. He didn't.

●

The days of dear old Badminton getting half an hour from Basingstoke Town Hall are dead and gone.

   John Bromley ITV Head of Sport, on the changes in TV coverage being brought about by the opening up of competition.

●

Why should I buy cricket? Nobody watches it.

   Greg Dyke, chairman of the ITV Network Sports Committee.

●

The Gold Medal – it's something they can't take away from you.

   Ben Johnson, Canadian sprinter, asked before the Seoul Olympics whether he would prefer a world record or the gold medal.

●

He's guilty because he's guilty.

   Juan Antonio Samaranch, President of the IOC, on Johnson after the sprinter failed a drug test. His gold medal was taken away from him.

●

From hero to zero in 9.79 seconds.

   Canadian graffito in the athletes village after Johnson's demise.

Canadian weightlifters: three clean and four jerks.

> Dressing-room graffito after 4 Canadian weight-lifters had been found guilty of drug-taking.

●

In the first game she was giving me three points with this careless attitude that had 'I can't win' written all over it. Then I remembered she was British.

> **Wendy Turnbull**, Australian tennis player, on Clare Wood.

●

We talk of British character and fighting spirit and tend to think it's old hat. But that's what sets British kids apart from the rest of the world and Daley Thompson has just given one of the best examples imaginable.

> **Frank Dick**, England athletics coach, on the injured Thompson's performance in Seoul.

●

Wogan makes us sick. Five seconds under water would probably kill him. I bet he couldn't swim along sideways for four yards with one leg sticking up vertical and pointing his toe.

> **Carol Hicks**, Britain's synchro team manager, reacting to gibes about her sport.

●

I'm thrilled and tonight in a bar somewhere I might be attempting another record.

> **Alister Allan**, British marksman, on setting a record and settling for Seoul silver behind Malcolm Cooper.

●

I am not particularly talented.

> **Kristin Otto**, winner of six swimming Olympic golds.

●

As long as I'm a drug-free zone, that's all I worry about.

> **Linford Christie**, promoted to silver after Johnson's disqualification.

He does not use drugs. If they said he was taking
roast chicken and baked potatoes then I would believe
that.

James Christie, Linford's father, before his son
was cleared of suspicion.

●

The other day someone said, 'Hey, have a cup of tea,'
and I had to say 'Hang on, let me read the writing on
the packet.'

Carl Lewis.

●

You don't have to be lovers to work well in a boat.

Dan Topolski on Holmes and Redgrave.

●

Stuff the silver.

Lennie 'Lawrie' Lawrence, coach to Aussie
Duncan Armstrong, swimmer who put Matt Biondi
in the shade.

●

I must have killed a nun.

Vinnie Smith after a difficult time in the world
angling championships.

●

This is one of the worst tragedies I have seen in
six and a half years on the federal bench. You have
it all, then enters greed and the whole thing seems to
go down the toilet.

Judge J. Lawrence Irving to David Jenkins
at his trial in San Diego where he was jailed
for trafficking steroids.

●

It's a sad day when the idol of yesterday takes off
his running shoes and we find he has feet of clay.

Sir Arthur Gold, chairman of the AAA, on
David Jenkins.

Ben Johnson used medical science to further his performance.

Jenkins, defending another Olympian besmirched by drugs.

●

This year was a fish. I throw it back.

Martina Navratilova.

●

Real men don't lob.

Runner's World magazine on George Bush's tendency to lob when playing tennis.

●

We had been playing excellent football, but we got outplayed. I sound like Mike Dukakis.

Bill Walsh, San Francisco 49ers coach.

●

Some guys reach for a drink in a crisis, I reach for a doughnut . . . I've never met a meal I didn't like.

Tommy Lasorda, LA Dodgers baseball manager.

●

The Miniature for Sport.

Spitting Image on Colin Moynihan MP.

●

The Sports Council cannot be regarded as a Social Security office.

Colin Moynihan.

●

It wasn't a working party, it was a nodding dog party. Moynihan said, 'This is what 'er indoors wants,' and they all nodded their heads in agreement.

Rogan Taylor, chairman of Supporters' Association, on ID cards.

●

I don't know who is in favour of the scheme unless you happen to walk along Downing Street and bump into the Minister.

Eddie Plumley, League executive Staff Association chairman.

It was like the Alamo out there. We had one shot,
but we shot the chief.
> **Eddie McCluskey**, Enfield manager, on against-
> run-of-play Cup win at Leyton Orient.

●

He ain't heavy, he's my brother.
> **Michael Dean Perry**, twenty stone brother of
> William 'Refrigerator', told to shed two stone by
> Chicago Bears.

●

Sammy Lee, Sammy Lee . . .
> Liverpool fans' chant after stocky infant in red
> ran on to retrieve the ball against Everton.

●

I have told my players never to believe what I say
about them in the papers.
> **Graham Taylor**, Aston Villa manager.

●

I've won what no one else but Bob Paisley has had
– permanent employment.
> **Brian Clough**.

●

At no time has it been our intention to operate
outside the League.
> **Philip Carter** before being deposed as League
> president.

●

That's not birdshit. That's Second Division chairmen
for you.
> **David Dein**, victim of a pigeon, eyeing the mess on
> his shoulder after being removed from the League
> management committee.

●

Mine is bigger than yours and I can prove it in court.
> **Stickers** in San Diego referring to size of New
> Zealand America's Cup boat.

●

Yeah, but I've got two.
> **Dennis Conner**'s spoof response.

I won't die at a football match. I might die being
dragged down the River Tweed by a giant salmon,
but not at a football match.

Jack Charlton, denying interest in the England
manager's job.

●

You'll all know when I finally quit rugby league –
they will put me on a boat, set it on fire, and send
it slowly down the Humber.

Fred Lindop, referee.

●

There is this caricature of rugby league players as
thick, thuggish and morose. They are far from that.
They are good company, intelligent and with a genuine
interest in the game.

Ian McCartney MP, forming an all-party RL
group in the Commons.

●

I'd like to think we'll accept decisions, but I won't be
surprised if the umpires go out of their way to be seen
to be unbiased. I wouldn't have thought they liked the
publicity over the Gatting affair, and I've got a feeling
Australia will feel a positive backlash.

Allan Border, Australian captain, dismissing
fears of Pakistani umpires before his side's tour.

●

What are you going to do if you feel you don't have a
chance? It is a conspiracy from the word go. The team
will do some rethinking and decide about the future of
the tour. If the management insist on completing the
tour then we will play under protest.

Allan Border, Australian captain, on Pakistani
umpiring after Australia lost the 1st Test in
Karachi by an innings and 188 runs.

●

We were never going to be allowed to win by fair
means. The team have voted in favour of stopping
the tour right now.

Allan Border as the Australians encountered

Pakistani umpires in the First Test. The tour continued.

●

We did not get one leg before decision. Pakistan got six. It seems strange.

Bobby Simpson, Australian coach, after Australia's defeat in Karachi.

●

We have outclassed the Australians. It would be cruel to suggest that victory was due to any reason other than our good performance.

Intikhab Alam, Pakistan manager, rejecting Australian protests about the umpiring, Karachi.

●

The Welsh Rugby Union souvenir shop is still open.

Cardiff Arms Park announcer after Wales's defeat by Romania.

●

When you come as a sponsor you are treated like royalty. I'd recommend it to anyone. When you come as a member on Test match Saturday you are shunted around as some species of sub-human.

Douglas Lever, Lancashire member and sponsor, on differing approaches at Old Trafford, 1988.

●

Sponsors are sponsors and if they become too powerful we could finish up in a situation where the sponsors are making the decisions.

Chris Peaker, Lancashire CCC treasurer recommending an increase in subscriptions as a way of members safeguarding their control in 1988. The attempt was rejected.

●

They are a good side, Denmark, but we had the better of things. I don't blame Gary Lineker for the defeat.

Bobby Robson after the England World Cup qualifying match with Sweden. The score was 0–0.

PLONKER
Sun headline in response to Robson's confusion.
•
IN THE NAME OF GOD, GO!
Daily Mirror headline after the Sweden match.
•
FOR THE LOVE OF ALLAH GO
Daily Mirror headline after the 1–1 draw with
Saudi Arabia in November.
•
I'm off to make some money. Phone me tomorrow.
Eric Hall, John Fashanu's agent, leaving the FA
hearing into Fashanu's scuffle with Viv Anderson
in the players' tunnel.
•
The West Indies pacemen have switched the attack
to me to the body. It's not very pleasant.
Allan Border explaining his heavy armour,
including chest protector in the Second Test
v West Indies in Perth.
•
We don't breed brutal cricketers.
Clive Lloyd, West Indies manager, rejecting
charges that his side played violent cricket.
•
We bowl short at them, they bowl short at us –
it's as simple as that.
Geoff Lawson, Australian paceman, as fast
bowlers got caught up in the bumper war, Second
Test in Perth. Lawson's jaw was broken by Curtly
Ambrose.
•
I'm certainly not ready to meet my maker. God gave
me this physical impairment to remind me that I am
not the greatest. He is.
Muhammad Ali on his fight against Parkinson's
disease.

1989

When you hear of something like the earthquake in
Armenia, you realise it's not a tragedy to lose a ski
race.
> **Vreni Schneider**, Swiss skier.

●

We should win but it won't be a landslide, just a
thoroughly professional performance.
> **Steve Ogrizovic**, Coventry City captain, before
> losing at non-League Sutton United in the FA Cup.

●

Fortunately our chaps are proper chaps and they
do have some intelligence. Therefore they are able
to countenance a multiplicity of set-plays suited to
the occasion.
> **Barrie Williams**, Kipling-quoting manager of
> Sutton's giant-killers.

●

I can't decide whether to go out and get drunk
or throw myself in the nearest canal.
> **Ian McNeill**, Shrewsbury manager, after Cup
> defeat by League's bottom team, Colchester.

●

It's not the board of directors who give away silly
goals and it's not the board who misses easy ones
at the other end.
> **Jim Smith**, Newcastle United manager, on 'Sack
> the Board' chants.

●

Losing still hurts, and that's good. When it stops
hurting, I'll stop playing.
> **Martina Navratilova** after losing to Helena
> Sukova in Australia.

This will break the link between football and hooliganism.

Colin Moynihan, Minister for Sport, introducing the Football Spectators Bill in Parliament.

●

At a stroke, Brian Clough has justified the Bill. If managers cannot control themselves it is hardly surprising that the sheep follow the shepherd.

Robert Adley, Tory MP for Christchurch, on the Nottingham Forest manager's televised ear-clipping of two pitch-invaders.

●

The Government is passing the buck of law enforcement from itself, the police and the courts to a quango.

Gordon Taylor, footballers' union leader.

●

Most of my trophies get out in the loft, but this one is special because you can't win it.

Eric Bristow on his MBE for services to darts.

●

I'd rather she [daughter Rachel] played tennis. Athletics is tainted – apart from the drugs, I hear kids talking about shoe contracts.

Daley Thompson.

●

Maybe I have been too honest, and kicked too many arses.

Ron Atkinson facing dismissal by Atletico Madrid.

●

Atkinson is only interested in making more money, having a good car and a villa on the beach.

Jesus Gil, Atletico president, before sacking him.

●

If the international set-up doesn't start treating players as human beings, Welsh rugby will end up as a nursery for rugby league.

Jonathan Davies, turning pro with Widnes.

Widnes, a wonderful blend of experienced stars and local youngsters like this lad Emosi Koloto.

Ray French, BBC rugby league commentator.

●

I just can't run around with the girls any more.

Wendy Turnbull, Australian tennis player, announcing her retirement.

●

I'm not a born-again Christian because I was never a Christian in the first place. In fact I've been a paid-up sinner all my life.

George Francis, Frank Bruno's trainer.

●

[Joe] Montana is not human out there. I don't want to call him a god, but he's somewhere in between.

Cris Collinsworth, Cincinnati Bengals player, on the San Francisco 49ers' Super Bowl-winning quarterback.

●

My father was a bricklayer and I used to help him. When you go out there and it's 100 degrees every day and you have your Pa tossing bricks, you learn to use your hands.

Jerry Rice, 49ers wide receiver and Super Bowl Most Valuable Player.

●

Barrie Williams came into our dressing-room and congratulated us. I don't know any poetry so I congratulated him back.

Dave Stringer, Norwich manager, on his team's 8–0 FA Cup win against Sutton.

●

Looks like I won't be on *Wogan* on Monday.

Lenny Dennis, Sutton striker.

●

Killing some of those giant eels is like killing a pensioner.

John Sidley, angler campaigning for protection of eels.

What about Eddie the bloody stupid Eagle?
Don't tell me he's a sportsman . . . thick as
two short planks.
   Eric Bristow defending darts as 'sport'.

I just did my best, and for once it was good enough.
  Hansjorge Tauscher, surprise world downhill
  ski-ing champion.

  •

I didn't want to rush it.
  Nigel Benn, British boxer, on his 67-second defeat
  of Mike Chilambe.

  •

You'll still hear him [Clough] in the directors' box.
  Stuart Gray, Aston Villa and ex-Forest player,
  on the manager's touchline ban.

  •

Laura's coming out for a couple of weeks, but I
shall have a headache.
  Frank Bruno at his training headquarters for
  the Tyson fight.

  •

He [Tyson] tried to take all his problems out on
Bruno. He saw other faces in front of him.
  Terry Lawless, the British heavyweight's man-
  ager, on mauling by Mike Tyson.

  •

The nearest player offside was at White Hart Lane.
  John Docherty, Millwall manager, on his team's
  disallowed goal at Highbury.

  •

It was clear that steroids were worth approximately
a metre at the highest levels of sport.
  Charlie Francis, Ben Johnson's coach.

  •

You spend a week here, enjoy yourself and at the
end you get paid a lot of money.
  Yannick Noah, French tennis player, in Cali-
  fornia.

  •

The only team we beat was Western Samoa. It was
a good job we didn't play all of Samoa.
  Gareth Davies, Welsh rugby union player, on
  his country's poor run before beating England.

Desert Orchid can't say he's as sick as a parrot, or that he won't be quoted until you've talked to his agent. As a gelding he is unlikely to make the nookie sections of the tabloids. He just sets off towards the fences and invites you to throw your spirit with him.

    Brough Scott, racing journalist.

●

We're aggressive, and we're competitive, but we can't all be Desert Orchids and loved by everyone.

    Bobby Gould, Wimbledon manager.

●

If there was any athlete not on them, they were probably from Sri Lanka or Timbucktoo or some other God-forsaken place.

    Jamie Astaphan, Ben Johnson's doctor.

●

People must think I spent the summer with Ben Johnson's doctor.

    Paul Ackford, London policeman and British Lions rugby player, on his dramatic season.

●

One player said half of Glasgow hates you and the other half reckons they own you.

    Frank McAvennie on leaving Celtic for West Ham.

●

Venables refused to concede that he will not make a move for Gary Lineker.

    Daily Mirror.

●

When Stearsby is quiet in his box, I get worried. When he's really evil I know he's in good form. He nearly had somebody's finger off yesterday, which is a good sign for Saturday.

    Gerald Ham, trainer, on his horse, one of the Grand National favourites.

210

It shows me there is still a spark in the fire. I've only got to throw a log on it.

Lee Trevino, veteran US golfer, on his opening 67 in the US Masters.

•

We stopped off for gas in Hicksville and they were saying 'Is it him? It is him, isn't it?' It was a nice feeling.

Nick Faldo, British golfer, after winning the US Masters.

•

Ever since I stopped wanting to become a nurse I wanted to be a jockey.

Tarnya Davis, the only woman rider in the Grand National.

•

His sister, our Elizabeth, is forever reminding him that he is ridiculously overpaid.

Brian Clough, on his son Nigel, the Nottingham Forest centre-forward.

•

Nobody gives a damn about technique here any more. It's all up-and-unders. Some of the matches I've watched this season have been worse than having teeth pulled.

Keith Burkinshaw, ex-Tottenham manager on his departure from Gillingham.

•

It's no more dangerous than driving up a motorway.

Jonjo O'Neill, racehorse trainer, on why Becher's Brook should not be altered.

•

I don't want to change the character of the race at all, unless the character is to kill horses.

Peter Calver, racehorse trainer, disagreeing.

•

Like the new club blazer? Arrived this week, only we had to cut 'Wembley 1989' off the breast pocket.

Jim Mills, ex-Widnes forward, after his old club's

shock defeat by St Helens in the Cup semi-final.

●

Some of these players will not be appearing at
Wembley. I will have to decide whether some of
them are even good enough to train at Wembley.

Alex Murphy, St Helens rugby league club coach,
before Challenge Cup final.

●

Strange how a football ground can grab hold of
you. I came past The Valley tonight and found myself
staring at it. All those memories – we had to go back,
didn't we?

Roger Alwen, Charlton chairman, announcing
the club's proposed return from Selhurst Park.

●

The lad he tackled was limping at 100mph soon
afterwards.

John Docherty, Millwall manager, on Teddy
Sheringham's sending-off against Wimbledon.

●

Jimmy [White] has a flair for living. When he was
12 he was as worldly as a 40-year-old and as naive
as a four-year-old. Jimmy could work out a yankee,
but couldn't name the capital of France.

Barry Hearn, snooker promoter.

●

He is right on par with any Olympic athlete since
the beginning of sporting history.

Maurice Lindsay, Wigan rugby league club
chairman, on Ellery Hanley.

●

I played like a slow puncture.

John Parrott on losing World Snooker final to
Steve Davis.

●

If she'd been running cricket, England would have
been better off than they are.

Ted Dexter, former Tory candidate (defeated),
on Mrs Thatcher.

212

Real officer-class. Confront him with a firing squad
and he would decline the blindfold.

> **Pat Pocock**, ex-England cricketer, on the new
> captain, David Gower.

●

I heard a supporter shouting 'You're f-----g hopeless
Nevin.' It stabs you in the heart.

> **Pat Nevin**, Everton footballer.

●

Football is the one thing we did as a family, and
now we're not a family any more.

> **Trevor Hicks**, who tried vainly to save his daugh-
> ters with the 'kiss of life' after the Hillsborough
> disaster.

●

We were given an oxygen tank to help with resusci-
tation and it was empty. This is an absolute disgrace.

> **Dr Glyn Phillips**, spectator at Hillsborough.

●

They [the police] thought they were dealing with a
security problem, and it was comparatively late in
the day when they realized they had a major safety
problem. I don't know whether their minds have been
conditioned over the years to thinking that way.

> **Graham Kelly**, chief executive of the FA, after
> the tragedy.

●

We must move the fans' preferences away from the
ritual of standing on the terraces.

> **Graham Kelly**.

●

Those who say the fans wouldn't like it [all-seater
stadia] should ask the half-million who have stopped
attending whether they want to come back to stand.

> **Owen Luder**, architect, post-Hillsborough.

●

If an elephant had been trapped it would not have
been able to move.

> **Liverpool fan**, aged 66, at the Leppings Lane End.

The FA Cup isn't worth it. There is nothing worth one death, let alone nearly 100.
Kenny Dalglish, Liverpool manager.

●

Look after them Shanks – from all the lads at Kirkby.
Floral message at Anfield's Shankly Gates.

●

The saddest, most beautiful sight I have ever seen.
Kenny Dalglish on the scarves and flowers at Anfield.

●

Part of the reason I love all sport, from rugby to ski-ing, is to have, just occasionally, one of those truly sublime moments, a fleeting passage when you think you've emulated a hero you've seen on television, a Nastase, a Lyle, a Ballesteros or a Norman. Sport lets you ape them – even though their genius allows them to do it rather more times than you.
David Gower.

●

What do we expect from him? The usual at Real – to win everything.
Real Madrid spokesman on John Toshack's appointment as manager.

●

I'm delighted with my score and I won't beat my wife tonight.
Jack Nicklaus.

●

It's an outlet, an escape from the humdrum. There's nothing gives me such a kick. Well, nothing except vodka.
Angela Farley, England netball player.

●

I looked in the mirror and realised there is too much violence in the world. Most of which has been perpetrated on me.
Jake 'Raging Bull' La Motta, former American boxer.

I once had to sleep with my leg across the fridge door.
Bob Paget, boxing trainer, on fighter Sammy Reeson's weight problem.

●

I'll be hitting him with so many lefts that he'll be crying out for me to hit him with a right.
Nigel Benn before fight with Michael Watson – who won.

●

They play in a certain way which is not my way. We have to give them a bit of credit, but we have to look at ourselves for the reasons we lost.
Kenny Dalglish, Liverpool manager, after Arsenal had beaten them with a last-minute goal in the last match of the season to take the title.

●

It's hard work making batting look effortless.
David Gower

●

We're all crackers to stand here for six and a half hours a day, but cricket's my life.
Dickie Bird, Test umpire.

●

Was I pushed or did I jump? Let's just say I saw the edge coming.
Dave Butz, Washington Redskins American footballer, on his retirement.

●

Maybe I should read my own book. I am not happy with my game.
Ian Woosnam, author of *Power Golf*.

●

After 18 years I am being beaten by teenagers. I just can't cope with these girls on clay with their heavy top-spin.
Chris Evert, veteran US tennis player, threatening retirement.

The axiom with track and field athletes was: if you don't take it, you don't make it.

Jamie Astaphan, Ben Johnson's doctor, to federal drugs inquiry in Canada.

●

If Canada wants to submit a team running clean, there should be two types of meeting – a clean one and an unclean one.

Jamie Astaphan.

●

Nobody told me. They were happy making all this money.

Ben Johnson, professing ignorance about the dangers of steroids.

●

Having called for a runner, [Ian] Healy then set off slightly quicker than Ben Johnson. Not a very convincing Oscar performance.

David Gower, suffering at the hands of the Australians.

●

It's the first female streaker we've had here. I've only seen that sort of thing at Twickenham before, but I thought ours was better.

Colonel John Stephenson, secretary of the MCC.

●

I saw her from the balcony and just happened to have my binoculars with me.

Paul Jarvis, England bowler at Lord's.

●

He's committed to us. We're committed to him. Probably we should all be committed.

Gregg Lukenbill, Sacramento Kings basketball club owner, on renewing coach's contract after 93 defeats in 142 games.

●

I'd sooner beat England with Ian Botham playing. If we do win at Headingley, you can bet that Both will tell us it would never have happened if he had been playing.

Allan Border, during summer of Test victories over England.

●

What do you think the chances are of your putting that cigar out?

John McEnroe to spectator at Beckenham.

I should have said: 'You cannot be serious.'

Brian Wilcox, the spectator.

●

In Don Revie's day he would not have got through the door, let alone pulled on a Leeds shirt.

John Giles, ex-Leeds player, on Vinnie Jones's £650,000 transfer from Wimbledon to Leeds.

●

Person you would most like to meet: Mike Tyson, any time, anywhere.

Vinnie Jones in Leeds programme profile.

●

He [Ben Johnson] has so changed his physique that, even if he never used drugs again, he would retain all the innate benefit of all the steroids he has used.

Sir Arthur Gold, chairman of the British Olympic Association.

●

Ben is the best sprinter I ever had. No one can question his ability.

Jamie Astaphan, Johnson's doctor.

●

It should not have surprised anyone that he was using steroids. You don't go from 10.17 to 9.83 on unleaded gas.

Jamie Astaphan.

●

It's like making love every time I get on the horse.

Willie Carson on riding Derby winner Nashwan.

Chang and this Agassi are getting away with murder.
They show no respect for the top guys. I'd like to start
a committee of veteran players to put these guys in
their place.
John McEnroe.

●

If you asked Jack Charlton to change Ireland's tactics
after winning 10 on the trot, he'd put you on the end
of his line, weight it heavily, and hurl you into a river.
Bobby Robson, England manager, answering
demands for experimentation.

●

What are you, a cricket player?
John McEnroe, berating himself at the Wirral
tournament.

●

You can remember me any way you want to – I
don't really care to be honest.
Jimmy Connors to the press after Wimbledon
defeat by unheralded Dan Goldie.

●

It's good when the cricket's on TV. The other guys
don't like it – especially the English.
John Fitzgerald, Australian tennis player at
Wimbledon.

●

If Chang wins Wimbledon, I'll drop my shorts on
Centre Court.
John McEnroe.

●

I think John is more relieved than I am.
Chang, after his defeat in the fourth round.

●

I'd be really shocked if I came back next year. It
would take a transplant.
Chris Evert.

It's rather like life. It has a habit of kicking you
in the groin, and we're all better people for it.

> **Finlay Calder**, British Lions rugby union coach,
> after Test defeat in Australia.

●

We went on a talk show together this morning.
In 1980 you couldn't get us in the same apartment
building.

> **Sugar Ray Leonard** on his next opponent, old
> foe Roberto Duran.

●

If I could turn the clock back 20 years, I'd have
picked a career in golf instead.

> **Ted Dexter**, chairman of England cricket selectors,
> during a summer of defeats by Australia.

●

It's all right for someone like Angus Fraser, Middlesex
and England bowler with no mortgage or kids, but I've
got a £66,000 mortgage and I'm £5,000 overdrawn.

> **Paul Jarvis**, Yorkshire and England cricketer,
> on why he decided to join 'rebel' tour to South
> Africa.

●

They disgust me. They should not be allowed to show
their faces in the sports arenas on Britain again. They
have betrayed black sportspeople and black people in
Britain.

> **John Regis**, black British athlete, on black crick-
> et 'rebels' Roland Butcher and Phillip DeFreitas,
> before they pulled out of the tour.

●

They can get £20,000 for having their heads knocked
off in the West Indies or £60,000 for two tours of South
Africa.

> **Jack Bannister**, Players' Association secretary,
> on the choice likely to be facing England players.

Nelson Mandela 26 not out.

> Banner held up in front of South Africa tour
> captain Mike Gatting at Lord's.

●

A few days ago John Carlisle and Norris McWhirter
were in court, arguing about principles. They spoke in
high falutin' terms about freedom. It's a pity that they
don't set equality of races as high as the freedom of 300
county cricketers.

> **Peter Roebuck**, cricketer-journalist.

●

If I couldn't fight this thing through, I'd go off and
sell insurance.

> **David Gower**, England cricket captain, during
> 4–0 series defeat by Australia.

●

I had to go off the circuit twice to avoid him. I
don't know what he's doing in Formula One racing.
He should be on the beach.

> **Thierry Boutsen**, grand prix driver, on Rene
> Arnoux.

●

I wrote to my wife before the match telling her that
I was retiring. I'd better get back to the hotel and get
the letter out of the post.

> **Finlay Calder**, British Lions rugby union captain,
> after Test victory in Australia.

●

I've got a career that depends a lot on being tall
and blonde, and if I ended up growing a beard I don't
think it would do me much good.

> **Sharon Davies**, British swimmer and model, on
> why she does not take drugs.

●

It's very important to arrive here early. The only
player who didn't and won was Tony Lema, and he
was still drunk from the champagne he had on the
plane coming over.

> **Tom Watson**, American golfer, at The Open.

It's altogether quieter, more reflective, less contro-
versial and more physical.

> **Sebastian Coe** on politics during his quest for
> a Conservative nomination.

●

Yesterday I was walking on water – today I needed
someone to show me how to play out of it.

> **Andrew Murray**, Manchester golfer, struggling
> in the Lancome Trophy after his European Open
> win.

●

Yanks rate Arsenal as exciting as a slice of cold pizza.

> Headline in the *Evening Standard* on the English
> champions' impact in Florida, where they were
> playing a friendly.

●

It's a complete fabrication. You can run that story
[Johnston for Rangers] for 10 years and it still wouldn't
be true.

> **Bill McMurdo**, Johnston's agent.

●

Rangers don't sign Catholics. Anyway, I don't want
to go to Ibrox.

> **Mo Johnston**, claiming he wished to stay in
> France after Celtic deal mysteriously collapsed.

●

I'm thrilled – I'm joining one of the biggest, probably
the biggest club in Europe.

> **Mo Johnston** on signing for Rangers.

●

116 years of tradition ended.

> Message on wreath delivered to Ibrox by Protestant
> traditionalists.

●

The world of Scottish football was rocked to its
pre-cast concrete foundations over the close season
when Rangers finally broke with over 100 years of

tradition and bought a player from FC Nantes for the first time in their history.

> ***The Absolute Game***, Scottish football fanzine.

●

A dream has come true.
> **Mo Johnston** on apparently rejoining Celtic from Nantes.

We are very pleased Paul has committed his future to West Ham, where he has been since a very young age. It's the kind of loyalty most players who come up through the junior ranks have for the club.

> **John Lyall**, West Ham manager, in April, after Paul Ince pledged to stay even if the club were relegated.

●

Paul is a Manchester United fan and Bryan Robson is his hero.

> **Ambrose Mendy**, Ince's agent, in August, during transfer negotiations with United.

Alex Ferguson wants Paul Ince for United like
Solomon wanted Sheba.
Ambrose Mendy in September.

●

Two over-used football 'facts': It is every schoolboy's
dream to play for Manchester United; West Ham play
attractive football.
Just Another Wednesday, Sheffield Wednesday
fanzine.

●

It is as hard as it looks. To try and have fun and
ride your ass off is difficult.
Wayne Rainey, Californian motor-cyclist.

●

BEARDO DUMPS FROGS!
Daily Star headline on alleged rebuff for French
club Marseille from Liverpool footballer Peter
Beardsley.

●

This means more than all the world records and
gold medals we've won over the years.
Frank Dick, director of coaching, on Britain's
European Athletics Cup triumph.

●

I'm drunk on adrenalin.
Michael Knighton, prospective Manchester Unit-
ed owner, after going on pitch before game with
Arsenal and shooting ball into Stretford End goal.

●

It is equivalent to giving someone the right to buy
your house and to live in it a couple of months to see
if they like it.
David Murray, Rangers chairman, cricitising
United chairman Martin Edwards' behaviour in
the Knighton deal as 'naive' as the takeover hit
snags.

Goliath has been well and truly toppled. They will be
stamping on his body, waving flags and shouting 'ha,
ha, ha'.

Howard Wilkinson, Leeds manager, after his
costly side's 5–2 defeat at Newcastle.

●

There's too much optimism around here.

Trevor Francis, Queen's Park Rangers player-
manager, at start of season – three months before
he was dismissed.

●

A lot of hard work went into this defeat.

Malcolm Allison, former Manchester City, Sporting Lisbon and Crystal Palace manager, laughing
off poor result for Fisher Athletic. He also left
within three months.

●

ACID-CRAZY THUGS 'TALK TO SATAN'
Daily Mirror headline on England football fans
in Sweden.

●

Hitler didn't tell us when he was going to send
over those doodle bugs, did he?

Bobby Robson refusing to announce his team
in advance of the World Cup qualifying match in
Sweden.

●

The ball had great red marks on it whenever I
headed it. It was like that film, *Nightmare on Elm
Street*.

Terry Butcher, England footballer, after his
blood-spattered performance in the World Cup
tie in Sweden.

●

This was good for me but not good for me. I had a tear.

Zina Garrison, American tennis player, on the
win that effectively ended Chris Evert's long career.

Win, lose or draw, I'm determined to enjoy myself.

> **Steve Coppell**, Crystal Palace's Merseyside-born manager, before League match at Liverpool.

●

This is something we'll never forget. It's left me numb. I've never seen Liverpool do that to any team before, and it's a terrible crime that we can't unleash them on the rest of Europe. I've never been involved in a defeat like that, even in primary school.

> **Steve Coppell** after a 9–0 defeat.

●

I don't know what he was used to, but he thinks Widnes is a wonderful place.

> **George Sadler**, secretary of Simms Cross Amateur Rugby League Club, on his Tongan discovery, Boblin Tuavao.

●

Not many people in Batley speak Latin, so the first thing we did was change the motto.

> **Stephen Ball**, chairman of Batley Rugby League Club.

●

The only thing that can stop the Oakland A's now is an earthquake.

> **Radio reporter** at baseball's World Series in San Francisco just before devastating tremors hit the city.

●

I look into their eyes, shake their hand, pat their back and wish them luck, but all the time I am thinking: 'I'm going to bury you.'

> **Seve Ballesteros**

●

Ayrton [Senna] has a small problem. He believes he can't kill himself because he believes in God.

> **Alain Prost** on the two motor-racers' dangerous rivalry.

I gather all that was to arrest one bloke. Must
have been Reggie Kray.

Jim Smith, Newcastle manager, on police 'over-
reaction' to crowd trouble at West Ham.

•

We don't know how to celebrate. I've given them
a bollocking through force of habit.

Ron Atkinson during a wretched run for Sheffield
Wednesday.

•

CLOUGHIE GRABBED MY GOOLIES
Headline in *The Sport*.

•

SOCCER STAR CUT OFF MY KITTY'S PRIVATES
Headline in *The People*. Player involved in the
alleged cat-castration was a Leeds reserve.

•

Every time I go through a lean spell I've lost a
yard. Every time I score a goal it means I'm over
the hepatitis.

Gary Lineker after his first hat-trick for Tottenham.

•

They [West Ham] didn't exactly have three girls
at the back either.

Howard Wilkinson, Leeds manager, defending
his team's alleged 'physical' approach.

•

We're not concerned with any bridges being built in
South Africa so much as ensuring that our own are
not destroyed.

Clive Rowlands, president of the Welsh Rugby
Union, severing links with South Africa.

•

I have torn Wales from my heart. My wonderful
memories, including my first international at Cardiff
Arms Park, are now sour. The Welsh will crawl in
future.

Dr Danie Craven, president of SA Rugby Board.

An arsenic . . . a large one.
> **Terry Venables**, Tottenham manager, ordering a drink after 4–1 home defeat by Chelsea.

●

The last time we got a penalty at home Christ was a carpenter.
> **Lennie Lawrence**, Charlton manager.

●

My oldest daughter is older than some of the lads I play with.
> **Tommy Hutchison**, Swansea City footballer, making his European debut at 42.

●

We have had no threats of that kind from Mrs Thatcher.
> **Tony Jacklin**, captain of Europe's golfers, on hearing that President Bush had hosted a lunch for the US Ryder Cup squad.

●

I was a saleable commodity and I believe I was exploited. Daddy only saw dollars when he looked at me.
> **Zola Budd**.

●

Ben Johnson is treated as the greatest bastard the world has seen, but for me he remains Olympic champion for the good reason that you will never make a thoroughbred from a mule, whatever you inject him with.
> **Dr Francois Bellocq**, advocating use of steroids for athletes.

●

I was very lucky I was caught.
> **Ben Johnson**.

●

Sometimes footballers are not perfect.
> **Vinnie Jones**, Leeds 'hard man', on *Wogan*.

Poland 0, England 0, though England are now looking better value for their nil.

Barry Davies, BBC football commentator, at World Cup qualifier.

●

WE CAN HAMMER WEDNESDAY!

Local paper headline, quoting Aldershot manager Len Walker, before his team's 8–0 home defeat by Sheffield Wednesday in the Littlewoods Cup.

●

I've been trying to be a footballer and that isn't me. I got a bit carried away with the Wogan show and all that.

Vinnie Jones.

●

I've taken a lot of stick. The lads are calling me 'Lurpak' – the best butter in the world.

Steve Hampson, Great Britain and Wigan rugby league player, sent off for 'nutting' a New Zealander.

●

I didn't commit a high tackle – a 5ft 4in player ran into me.

Gary Hetherington of Sheffield Eagles rugby league club, on receiving an eight-match ban.

●

Bill Bell: Chairman and business entrepreneur, dedicated to making Port Vale the No.1 team in the Potteries. Bill also wants to find the Lost City of Atlantis, be the first man to walk the Channel, and skateboard up Mount Everest.

The Oatcake, Stoke City fanzine, 'derby match' issue.

●

My God – if I'm Britain's No.1 it's pretty bad really.

Jo Durie, ranked 105th among world's women tennis players.

Perhaps if it had been at The Kop or the Stretford End it would have been given – but not at the Sainsburys End.

> **Steve Coppell**, Crystal Palace manager, on being refused a penalty.

●

You're going home in a military ambulance.

> Swindon fans' taunt to visiting Bolton supporters during ambulance workers' dispute.

●

Actually I tried to buy Monaco but I found that some guy called Rainier had got there first.

> **Ken Bates**, Chelsea chairman, recalling his tax exile in Monte Carlo.

●

If you have 11 Yorkshiremen giving 100 per cent, then who have you to be frightened of?

> **Steve Oldham**, appointed Yorkshire cricket manager after another poor season and autumn in-fighting.

●

He's only a racehorse. We can always get beaten.

> **David Elsworth**, Desert Orchid's trainer, after the great steeplechaser lost at Sandown.

●

These All Blacks were undoubtedly the most ignorant, arrogant bunch I've come across in rugby. We were virtually licking their backsides . . . but they were only interested in beating the hell out of us then getting out as fast as possible.

> **Gordon Pritchard**, Pontypool coach, on Wayne Shelford's New Zealand rugby union tourists.

●

There's a few people's legs I'd like to have broken, people like Jarvis [Astaire], [Micky] Barrett, [Mickey] Duff – but they're still walking around aren't they?

> **Frank Warren**, sporting entrepreneur, laughing off 'gangster' image, months before he was shot.

There is no league table in libel. No First Division, no Second Division and no Vauxhall Conference.

> **Justice Michael Davies** directing the jury with regard to the financial reparation for Lord Aldington, ex-Tory Party chairman.

●

After I've beaten Gary Mason I'll be looking for Tyson. He can't hide behind Don King's hairdo forever.

> **Mark Wills**, American heavyweight, before losing to Britain's Mason.

●

The draw was made just for the fun of the television audiences.

> **Diego Maradona** complaining that the World Cup draw had been fixed.

●

The most stupid thing said by a footballer in the eighties.

> **FIFA spokesman** on Maradona's claim.

●

Of course they want him back. Just imagine the TV audience they will get the next time Johnson runs against Carl Lewis.

> **Steve Ovett** on moves by IOC members to cut short Ben Johnson's sentence for drugs.

●

There is a need for clubs to become more professional. Who knows, in a few years' time we could be known as Ford Harlequins, with advertising on our jerseys.

> **Colin Herridge**, Harlequins rugby union club secretary.

●

There is a stable door slightly ajar. Outside the stable door, eight members of the International Board are scrummaging furiously, trying to keep the door closed. Inside are the Scots and the Irish, but every other horse has bolted.

> **Finlay Calder**, Scotland and British Lions captain, on the spread of professionalism in rugby union.

Within a decade every top team will field four fast bowlers pitching short with no one in front of the bat. Adventurous batting will be reserved for one day games. Ruthlessness and violence will be indistinguishable.

Peter Roebuck, cricketer-journalist in the *Sydney Morning Herald*.

●

I've left my parents behind, even lying to my brother that I was going to see a friend. I may never see them again and I don't know if they're safe. But today I think it has all been worthwhile.

Nadia Comaneci, Romanian gymnast, on defecting to the West.

●

The decade. I'm sick of reading about that. Look ahead. Forget the Eighties – the Nineties are going to be a more positive decade. We might clean up the world. We might even have cleaner tennis courts.

John McEnroe.

I'm going into the Nineties just working to keep in the game. I've got one big motivating factor – I've got nothing else to do.

Steve Davis after losing to Stephen Hendry in the UK Open snooker final.